DESTINY WALKING

THE 21 DAY FREEDOM CHALLENGE

ALICE KRUG

DEDICATION

I would like to dedicate this book to my family for allowing me the grace to discover my God-given identity. This book is a testimony to God's transforming power, His unchanging ways, and His perfect love, for the imperfect me.

To J.D. for standing firm and steadfast in the midst of every storm we've encountered through these last twenty years. I love you and am so thankful for the years we've shared and many more to come.

To Dad for teaching me how to live on purpose and to embrace life.

To Mom for reminding me (everyday if needed) to "stay the course" whether in my marriage, parenting teenagers, or going after my God-given dream.

To Grant and Dawson for teaching me how to love deeply, forgive without hesitation and to cherish every moment I'm given here on earth—you truly are a gift from God.

To Susan, my sister and friend, for weathering the storms that came our way and allowing God to redeem, repair and restore our relationship. We truly can say we've seen the hand of God at work in both our lives!

To my friend, Janie, for speaking truth into my life when I was ready to give up.

CONTENTS

CONTENTS

INTRODUCTION

Where the Spirit of the Lord is there is FREEDOM,
1 Corinthians 3:17.

Have you ever wondered if there is a destiny planned specifically for you? Do the events in our everyday lives simply unfold without rhyme or reason? Have you ever asked yourself or others the question, "What *is* destiny?" A few years ago, I struggled with that very question. I could not make sense of the unfortunate events that were taking place in my life. I didn't understand what was happening to me, or more importantly, *why*.

As I faced the questions that were shaking my faith to the core, God invited me to take a journey with Him—a journey to find the answers I so desperately needed. This journey with the Lord would require me to leave a place of comfort and enter into a land of endless possibilities. Although I didn't understand it at the time, God was preparing me to put these very words to paper as I retraced my steps with Him.

At the beginning of our journey together, God reminded me of the story of Abraham.

God had spoken to Abraham telling him to leave his hometown, his family and to go to a place He would show him. In **Genesis 12:1-4**, the Lord said to Abram, *Leave your country, your people and your father's household and go to the land I will show you,* (author's paraphrase). Abraham wasn't given a detailed itinerary of his trip—he was given *one* instruction—*to leave*. God asked

Abraham to leave all that was familiar; to trust Him to lead and guide him. You might be thinking, how did Abraham know where he was going and if he was even heading in the right direction? Abraham walked by faith. Although he did not know the details of where he was going—his trust was in knowing *The One* who was sending him.

My journey wasn't as extreme as Abraham's. God did not require a physical journey that caused me to leave my hometown. Instead, mine was a spiritual journey, one that required me *to leave the familiarity of my old self—my old thoughts, attitudes, and behaviors*—at the foot of the cross. In exchange for all my old baggage, He would give me *absolute truth*—which would ultimately transform everything I'd known to be true about myself.

I had no idea where this journey would lead, but with each step of faith, God began to reveal Himself to me. Through each struggle, God began to teach me what *resting in Him* looked like; and how to trust Him completely. God's desire for me was that *He* would become my *source of truth* and *provision*. God began a refining process within me; allowing the trials in my life to transform me. He was teaching me that who I was—my true identity—could only be found in *Him*.

Long before I took my first breath, my identity *in Him* had already been established; all I had to do was accept it and walk in it. I would no longer be defined by what the world or others thought—or identified by my own negative self-talk. My past mistakes and life experiences would no longer have the power to define me. I began to see that I was created in His image with a purpose that would only unfold as I walked closely with Him—allowing Him to unveil the *real* me.

Jesus calls all of His children to rest in Him. "Live in me. Make your home in me just as I do in you," **John 15:4** (MSG). It is only in God's presence that we can cease striving in our own strength and find rest for our weary souls. "Come to me, all you who are weary and burdened, and I will give you rest. Take my yoke upon you and learn from me, for I am gentle and humble in heart, and you will find rest for your souls. For my yoke is easy and my burden is light," **Matthew 11:28-30**.

The world changes daily—people's opinion of us can change daily—but the Word of God never changes. God is the only constant in our lives. "Jesus Christ is the same today, tomorrow and forever," **Hebrews 13:8**. It is as we rest in His presence that He reveals Himself to us, and gives us an identity that can never be changed, replaced or taken away.

Again I ask the question: What is destiny?

Destiny is a pre-determined course of events. Notice the word *pre-determined*. If something is pre-determined, it has been "thought of" first. The Bible says in **Jeremiah 1:5**, "Before I formed you in the womb I knew you, before you were born I set you apart." Before you were ever created, God says He knew you. He pre-determined who you would be, what you would look like and what purpose you would fulfill during the course of your life.

You are not here by accident; God created you—the real you—on purpose and with a plan in mind.

"For I know the plans I have for you; plans to prosper you and not to harm you, plans to give you a hope and a future," **Jeremiah 29:11**. The Bible clearly says that God has a plan and a purpose for His children—a destiny designed with you in mind. He has ordained all the events of your life and is present through each one.

Before you can understand your purpose and start walking toward your destiny, you must first understand the God who created you—and who He created *you* to be. Allow Him to become your source of truth. God sent His one and only Son to the cross to rescue you from the dominion of darkness and restore you back into relationship with Him. As you plug into that absolute truth, you will begin to understand your real identity, your value, and where you fit into this big picture called *life*.

What if for 21 days you took a journey that would connect you to the heart of God in a way that totally transformed your thinking?

Transformation occurs through a personal and intimate relationship with the Lord. We are forever changed when we hear the voice of God confirming to us the truth about our innermost being. When we hear the Creator say—*I knit you together in your mother's womb; I have plans to prosper you, giving you a hope and a future; you were chosen before the world began; you are fearfully and wonderfully made; you are unique, one-of-a-kind; my masterpiece! You* are mine; you are robed in righteousness—a child of The King!—it changes everything. One Word from God changes how you see yourself, how you see others, and how you see your circumstances. The truth of God's Word exposes the lies the enemy uses to deceive us into believing God isn't really there, or He must not care. The truth can soften the hardest heart, and for me, God's whisper can heal the deepest wounds—the ones you thought would destroy you.

What if you could see yourself, your circumstances, and others through the eyes of God?

The *21-Day Freedom Challenge* will connect your heart to the heart of God. You will gain an understanding of the incredible depth of God's love for you. When you know you are loved and experience that love; something shifts inside. We were all created by God and for God. We were created for genuine relationships with God and with others. But often there is something that holds us back from experiencing true fulfillment—from fully realizing an intimate relationship with God, our parents, our children, and our friends.

What keeps us from experiencing the abundant life and freedom the Bible so clearly says is yours and mine?

We have an enemy that we've unknowingly allowed access into our lives. The Bible says in, **1 Peter 5:8**, "Be sober, be vigilant; because your adversary the devil walks about like a roaring lion, seeking whom he may devour." We have listened to and agreed with the lies of the enemy. Those lies have been used to build walls—walls we hide behind, that have become our protection.

Other lies we have believed come from the unfortunate events that have taken place in our lives; labels others have placed on us, or the negative words we've spoken about ourselves. Satan wants to keep us blinded to this truth. The very walls we've built around our hearts for protection, keep us from our One True Protector, and an intimate relationship with Him.

What lies have you believed about yourself—from past events or what others that have said—that have become the walls you hide behind? Are there lies the enemy has whispered to you that are keeping you from experiencing God's best for your life?

It's time to tear down the walls that the enemy is using for your destruction, and allow the God Who created you to redefine your true identity!

Today is the day to take back the authority you've been given, and allow God to rebuild whatever the enemy has tried to destroy. Maybe it is an event in your life that has left you wounded, a relationship that's been damaged, or a dream that has died. God longs for His children to live abundant lives. You were not created to live in defeat! Allow God to take those old rags you've been wearing, and exchange them for the robe of righteousness—custom-made especially for you!

Destiny Walking is about moving forward in faith, connecting to the heart of God and discovering the *real you*—who you are in Christ. For the next 21 days, you will begin your journey toward destiny—a destiny created specifically for you. Begin by inviting God into those deep and guarded places in your heart. Those places where hurtful memories are stored, images are recorded and attitudes are developed—the place the enemy has used to convince you that you are less than God's best.

God wants to uproot the lies the enemy has planted in your heart and replace them with His truth. God's Word is the ultimate power source—a constant flow of power beyond anything you can ask, think, or imagine. It is time to unplug from the world's thinking and plug into God's truth! Open your heart wide and get ready to take a powerful journey with the One who knows you best— your transformation awaits you!

Alice Krug

DAY 1

STOLEN IDENTITY—
DISCOVERING THE REAL YOU

The thief comes only to steal and kill and destroy. I came that they may have life and have it abundantly, **John 10:10.**

The enemy comes to steal your identity, kill your dreams and destroy your relationship with God and with others. Jesus came to give you life—abundant life! It is time to claim what is rightfully yours, your identity in Christ—an identity that was purchased for you on the cross!

Your value is not measured by your past mistakes or the opinions of others.

Do you know your value? The value of something is determined or measured by how much a person is willing to pay for a particular item. God knew how much you were worth. He demonstrated your value by purchasing you with the blood of His only Son, Jesus Christ. You are a treasured child who belongs to God. *You matter!* You are a child of the living God; you are His *masterpiece*, and you were bought with a price, (**1 John 3:1; Ephesians 2:10; John 3:16**).

What's holding you back from walking in confidence and the truth of who God says you are? Is your acceptance dependent upon what others say? Who or what do you allow to define you? The opinions of others or your own past mistakes? What if I told you that nothing has the power to define you—unless you give it the power to do so?

I spent the majority of my life looking to others for acceptance, only to find their opinion of me changed daily. Once I realized looking to others for my approval was like chasing the wind, I would like to say that I started allowing God to tell me who I was, but that wasn't the case. I believed that if my acceptance didn't come from the opinions of others, then it most surely would come from my performance. I guess I don't have to tell you what that led to—striving for perfection. I'll let you in on a little secret; it's exhausting trying to attain perfection! As I soon found out, there is no such thing as perfect—unless of course you're God!

I worked hard at everything I did—playing sports; making good grades; wearing the perfect outfit—the list was endless. When I failed at something, I spent more time beating myself up than I had trying to succeed in the first place! I was caught up in a cycle of defeat that flowed into every area of my life. I never knew that my identity in Christ and His love for me was not based on my performance or accomplishments. That's definitely worth repeating, *Our identity in Christ and His love for us does not hinge on our performance or accomplishments.*

The enemy (Satan) knows how valuable you are, and he works daily to keep you blinded from the truth of who you are in Christ. He schemes and plans ways to gain access to your soul, which consists of your mind, your will, and your emotions. He attacks those areas because Satan knows how dangerous you are once you begin walking in the freedom, confidence, and the authority of your true identity. God wants the truth rooted in the deepest part of your heart—you are not defined by your performance, accomplishments, or past mistakes. Who you are is determined by your relationship with Him.

We have an enemy who uses our past mistakes as an opportunity to whisper lies and condemnation. Unfortunately, most of us unknowingly come into agreement with those lies and begin accepting them as the truth of who we really are. Our reality becomes based on the lies we've believed, rather than the truth of God's Word.

No matter what unfortunate circumstances have taken place in your life, or past mistakes you've made; you are NOT defined by your past! Satan is a liar and the Bible says, *there is no truth in him, he is the father of lies,* (**John 8:44**). Stop allowing the lies of the enemy to overshadow the truth of who you are in Christ. It is vital that you allow the One who created you to define you. God must become your source of truth. When your identity is rooted in Christ, you will stand with confidence no matter the opposition you face. When you allow God the final word regarding who He says you are, the opinions of others and the past lose the power they once had over you. **Your identity in Christ never changes and can never be take away from you. Once you are a child of God; you are always a child of God—no matter what!**

 Colossians 1:16 states, "all things have been created through Him and for Him." You and I were created by God and for God. He longs to have an intimate relationship with you. You can begin a relationship with Him by simply inviting Him into your heart. If you haven't asked Jesus into your heart, the time is now. "If you confess with your mouth that Jesus is Lord and believe in your heart that God raised him from the dead, you will be saved," **Romans 10:9** (NLT).

 If you're ready for your personal relationship with God and to step into your new identity, pray this simple prayer…

Dear Lord, I know that I have sinned against you. I repent and ask you to forgive me of all my sins. I believe that Jesus died on the cross for my sins and rose again. I surrender my will to you Jesus and ask you to come into my heart and be the Lord and Savior of my life. Thank you for saving me! AMEN

 Now that you have invited Jesus into your heart, you're a new creation, the old has gone! "Therefore, if anyone is in Christ, the new creation has come: The old has gone, the new is here!" **2 Corinthians 5:17.**

Are you ready to begin your journey with God? As you listen for the voice of God, He will reveal to you your new identity. Start by asking God a few questions. I've listed a few to get you started. In **John, Chapter 10**, the Bible says, *My sheep listen to my voice, and I know them, and they follow me.*

It's time to silence the shouts of the world and hear the whisper of God.

If you are a new believer in Christ, it's normal to have questions in the area of hearing God's voice. **2 Timothy 3:16-17** says that all Scripture is, *God-breathed.* Whether you've been a believer for many years or you are a new believer, the Bible is an excellent way to hear from God. As we close this chapter, I want you to experience God's love for you, and the best way to experience His unconditional love is to allow Him to speak His truth to your heart.

Find a quiet place and simply become aware of God's presence. You can start by asking God the questions below. Write down anything that the Lord puts in your heart.

LISTENING TO THE VOICE OF GOD:

1. God, do You love me?

John 3:16, "For God so loved the world, that He gave His only Son, that whoever believes in Him should not perish but have eternal life."

Romans 5:8, "but God shows His love for us in that while we were still sinners, Christ died for us."

2. God, what unique qualities have you given me; what makes me special?

3. God, show me any lies I've believed about myself or about events in my past. Would You show me the truth so that I can replace all the lies with the truth of Your Word?

Remember that what God says about you matters more than anyone else's opinion. God loves you and wants the very best for you. You belong to God and are accepted, not because of what you do, but because of what He has already done. You are God's child because He says so. You are here for such a time as this; not by accident, but on purpose—a purpose given by the God who loves you with an everlasting love.

TODAY'S DECLARATION:

I will remember that I am God's child; a masterpiece—my identity is not based on my performance, it's not determined by labels others may have placed on me—my identity is 100 percent based on God's love for me. I am God's child; created to do great things!

DAY 2

OVERCOMING INSECURITY—
IS YOUR HEAD GETTING IN THE
WAY OF YOUR HEART?

For years, I struggled with insecurity. At the ripe old age of twelve, insecurity knocked on the door of my heart. I was in the seventh grade when I decided I would try out for cheerleader. There were three spots for the taking, and I hoped I'd be chosen to fill one of those sacred spots. For the next few weeks, I practiced and prepared for the tryout. Tryouts came and went, and the day of selection was finally here. The whole school—yes, the *whole* school—gathered in the auditorium for the big announcement. I sat with my fingers crossed and my heart racing as the first name was called. It seemed like an eternity for them to call the second name—and still my name wasn't called. Could it be that my name would be the third and final name? I sat listening intently as they announced the third name of the girl that would be chosen to fill the last spot. You probably guessed it—my name was never called. I wasn't chosen.

My heart broke into a million pieces as I sat watching the three who were chosen celebrate their victory. At that moment, the enemy took the opportunity to fill my mind and heart with the lies that would catapult me into a cycle of defeat for years to come. The lies went something like this—*you're not good enough; you're not pretty enough; you're not popular enough*. Notice a common word used with each statement—*enough*. That day the lie was planted—*you are not enough!* Those four words would become the reality I would live out as my truth in the years to come.

Has there been a time in your life that you felt like you just didn't measure up? Maybe you too are familiar with the lie, *you are not enough?* The Bible says that you are created in His image (**Genesis 1:27**), and are fearfully and wonderfully made (**Psalm 139:14**), yet it is often easier to believe the opposite.

Doubt in what God has said keeps us from accepting His truth and walking in our God-given identity.

Self-image is a driving force in our society today. Just look at Facebook, Twitter, Instagram; not to forget the infamous *selfie*. Just the word *selfie* depicts the echo of the world which is screaming, *it's all about me*. Now, don't get me wrong. Who doesn't like posing for a picture with friends or capturing the moment? But, when there's an app available that allows you to filter and alter the way you look with the click of a button—we've got a problem. Where does the idea originate from that leads us to believe something is wrong with us? Why do we think we need to find a way to *make ourselves better*? Why isn't who we are or what we look like good enough?

With so many ideas and images shouting at us, telling us what beauty and success look like, it's no wonder we have an epidemic of low self-esteem and insecurity.

Maybe, like me, you've struggled with insecurity—a low opinion of yourself; lack of confidence; self-doubt. Insecurity keeps us from walking in the true identity of who God created us to be. Insecurity creeps in the moment you begin to compare who you are or your situation to those around you. When you look to anyone or anything other than God for your acceptance, insecurity rears its head—and causes you to go in search of something that will fill the void in your life and silence the voice that reminds you that *you are not enough*.

Have you ever picked up a magazine while standing in the grocery line, and after looking through the pages at all the *perfect* people, you walk away feeling like you need a complete makeover? The world splashes images all around us that exemplify their idea of perfection. We are told what's in style; the hottest haircut for the year; the coolest car to drive; the newest phone to purchase—the subliminal messages are never-ending.

As a woman, you are trying to measure up to what you see on the cover of a magazine—the model in the department store window (girls, you know the store), or if you're a guy, the life-size mannequin in the sporting goods store with bulging biceps and muscles that can be counted through the skin-tight Nike dry-fit shirt!

If we are honest, we have all had moments where we've struggled with the thoughts of wanting to *fit in* and look the part. We question if we're okay just the way we are or if there is something we can change to help us better fit into the mold of this world. The Bible says, "Do not conform to the pattern of this world, but be transformed by the renewing of your mind," **Romans 12:2**. The truth of God's Word says, *we are uniquely made and are a masterpiece* (**Ephesians 2:10**, NLT). Think about what a masterpiece is to an artist. It's unique, one-of-a-kind, and it's the absolute best piece of work an artist can create. That's exactly how God sees you.

How do you see yourself? What image of yourself do you hold in your heart? When you look in the mirror, what do you see? What do you say to the person you see in the mirror when no one is listening? For me; there were many years when I didn't like myself. I began to compare myself to those around me at an early age. I never felt that I measured up. I was loud, outspoken, athletic—not your typical girly-girl. As I got older, those thoughts stayed—as well as the comparison that came with them. I began to come into agreement with the one (Satan) telling me those lies. The more I agreed, the deeper those lies rooted themselves into my heart.

One day the Lord began speaking to me about comparison.

I began to see that I was comparing myself—my looks, performance, and abilities—with others. I was using the looks, performance and abilities of others to measure my own self-worth. Because I often fell short, my own insecurities were, in turn, sabotaging my relationships. Instead of looking to God, I was looking to the people in my life for acceptance and approval.

Comparing myself to others kept me focused on the *external* instead of the *eternal*. When you begin to look to God for your acceptance and approval, you will find that it doesn't require your performance or perfection, but rather your faith. You simply believe what God's Word says about you, and use that as your mirror. The question is, *Are you reflecting what the world defines as beauty or who God is?* I heard it said, *true freedom comes when you no longer feel the need to impress others around you.*

There's nothing more freeing than when you step out of the world's definition of beauty and success; and step into the transforming power of God's righteousness!

If you are ready to experience God's transforming power, pray this simple prayer with me today.

Dear God, please forgive me for comparing myself to those around me. I know that I am created perfectly in Your image. You have a plan and a purpose for my life. God, reveal what is in my heart that is causing me to feel insecure about myself. Whatever lie that I've believed about myself, show me the truth about how You see me.

I am fearfully and wonderfully made; I know that full well, (**Psalm 139:14**).

LISTENING TO THE VOICE OF GOD:

1. Ask the Lord if there are any lies you have been believing about yourself.

2. Ask God: would You give me a picture of what enough looks like to You?

3. Can you think of a time when you compared yourself to someone you knew or maybe you didn't know? What thoughts crept into your mind?

4. List anything about yourself you have a hard time accepting. Ask God to reveal the truth about all the things you have listed. Write down everything God reveals to you.

TODAY'S DECLARATION:

I will stop comparing myself to those around me and I will thank God for my unique qualities. I will celebrate each day the gifts and abilities that God has purposefully placed inside of me.

DAY 3

JEALOUSY—IT'S NOT FAIR; I WANTED THAT!

Jealousy has been around from the very beginning of time. **Ezekiel 28:12-17**, describes Satan as an exceedingly beautiful angel. He was the highest of all angels, the most beautiful of all of God's creations, but he was not content in his position—Satan desired to be God. Satan wanted what someone else had, and it was his desire for more that sparked a fire of jealousy and created a mess for us all!

Another story of jealousy arose between Cain and Abel, (**Genesis 4:8**). Cain's jealousy drove him to do the unthinkable— murder his brother, Abel. This was the first murder recorded in human history, all because of one man's jealousy toward another. Let's not forget the story of Joseph. Joseph was the second to the youngest of twelve sons. Joseph's father favored him and this made his older brothers extremely jealous of him. They became so jealous of Joseph that they sold him into slavery and then told his father he had been killed by a wild animal, (**Genesis 37**).

Jealousy arises when we want something we think we deserve, or when we want something we don't have but *think* we need. Jealousy is not something we like to admit, so we keep it hidden in our hearts. Jealousy is the root cause of many of the relational problems we experience.

You are still worldly. For since there is jealousy and quarreling among you, are you not worldly? Are you not acting like mere humans? **1 Corinthians 3:3**.

Can you think of a time when you have been jealous?

Have you scrolled through Facebook, Twitter, or Instagram and come across *that* girl? She's got the looks, the brains, the athletic ability—*and* she has hundreds of followers! Every picture she posts is flawless—like it's been airbrushed! People seem to flock to her everywhere she goes.

Most guys don't want to admit it, but they also have insecurities that creep in from time to time. Being a man does not make you exempt from feeling insecure. I remember our son coming home from middle school and high school to tell us about his day. The stories were always entertaining—especially when it came to the locker room "talk" and comparisons. I'll spare you the details! From the youngest age, the things said about us and done to us have a long-lasting impact.

Men and women, young and old—we have all wrestled

with thoughts of jealousy. What ignites these feelings? Why is it so hard to be happy when something good happens to others? What causes us to judge others based on what we see externally when we don't even know them—and then make the decision that we don't like them?

These questions are easy for me to answer because there was a time in my life that jealousy consumed me. I disliked anyone I *thought* had more than me, was prettier than me or their athleticism outshined mine. Yes, I confess, that was me—completely consumed with jealousy! What about you? Has someone you know received what you wanted—an award you thought you deserved; a spot on a team that you didn't make; a material possession you were saving for; the girlfriend/boyfriend who broke up with you for another? How did that make you feel?

Yesterday we talked about comparison and how it fuels jealousy and feeds your insecurity. Remember, insecurity is a lack of confidence in your identity. Insecurity causes you to doubt yourself; questioning whether or not you are good enough. Insecurity feeds jealousy and has a way of hardening your heart and manipulating your mind.

In my younger years, I often perceived the strengths and abilities of others as a threat, rather than the gift another was given. As I matured, graduated high school and went off to college, the jealousy not only followed, but continued to grow. Not understanding what was happening, I became distant and closed off to other people. The prettier the girl, the more I disliked her. The smarter the girl, the more stupid I felt. And, if she was athletic, the more competitive and driven to perfection I was. It isn't a bad thing to want to look good or do your best. But, the driving force or the motivation needs to be called into question if you are striving in an unhealthy way to achieve something or become something God never intended.

God will never assist us in becoming someone else—but He will always assist us in becoming the best we can be through Him!

For years, jealousy fed my insecurity and became the driving force behind the perfectionism in my life. I never felt *good enough*. I always believed that others were better and I was *less than*. The worse I felt about myself, the harder I tried to measure up. The enemy used every opportunity of comparison to offer up lies—lies that fanned the fire of the jealousy that burned within. Jealousy caused me to question my identity, bringing about a deep insecurity. This insecurity kept me from walking in the confidence of who God said I was. The more I compared myself or my circumstances to others, the more I fed the jealousy—and the more inadequate I became in my own mind.

There is a word that I want to explore that just might be the key to your freedom in the area of jealousy. The word is—*appears*. Let me explain. When you view others and their situations through your natural eyes, you will only see what appears to be the truth of the matter. Something that appears one way to you could be something else entirely.

What if something you perceive as truth is really a deception from the enemy? Deception is another trick the devil uses to keep your God-given identity hidden from you—and one of his most valuable tools. The word deceived means: *to cause to wander from safety, truth or virtue.* Deception starts in your mind, and this is where the enemy first attacks.

Your mind is the battleground where the enemy wages war.

When a believer has been deceived, they begin to drift away from the truth of God's Word, and toward the lies of the enemy. Jealousy comes from the deceptive thoughts that take your focus off God's truth and place it on yourself. You either begin to believe that you are not good enough—or that others are so much better than you. Satan knows that you are the most vulnerable when it comes to your identity. Your identity in Christ is where you are the biggest threat to the enemy. Understanding what jealousy is and where it comes from will help you use your authority to overcome those jealous feelings and begin to walk in the truth.

First, you must **plug into the power source—God's Word**. As you begin to allow the truth of God's Word to fill your heart, the lies of the enemy are exposed. It's so important to spend time with God, allowing Him to search your heart. One of my favorite verses in the Bible is found in **Psalm 139:14**, "I praise you because I am fearfully and wonderfully made; your works are wonderful, I know that full well." In this passage, David is praising God for how he was created. As God began to teach me who I was in Him, a big part of the lesson became understanding how those lies I held in my heart blocked the truth—the truth that I was fearfully and wonderfully made!

Psalm 139:23, 24 goes on to say, "Search me, O God, and know my heart; test me and know my anxious thoughts. See if there is any offensive way in me and lead me in the way of everlasting." After praising God, David made a request. He asked God to look into his heart; to see if there was anything hindering his relationship with God or with others. David wanted to know if he was holding onto any lies from the enemy and he wanted to expose any thoughts that were not in agreement with God's truth. That's a pretty bold prayer if you ask me. Yet, it is one of the most important things we can ask God to reveal to us—the truth about what's really in our hearts. When we allow God to search our hearts, the enemy's lies are exposed and room is made for the truth to be revealed.

Jeremiah 17:9-10a states, "The heart is deceitful above all things and beyond cure. Who can understand it? I the Lord search the heart and examine the mind..." God is the only One who truly knows the condition of your heart. David understood that a pure heart kept him close to God. It is God's truth that exposes those places in your heart that are keeping you from walking closely with Him.

Second, we must **stop comparing ourselves**—our appearance or abilities—as well as our circumstances or positions to those around us. God has created each of us uniquely with our individual gifting and abilities. Do you know that there are no two fingerprints alike? God put a fingerprint on you when He knit you together in your mother's womb. You are created in His image. God has intricately woven into you His very spirit. David knew how special he was despite any hardships he endured in his life. He never lost sight of the truth that He was accepted, chosen and loved by God. When we accept who we are based on God's truth we will walk about in confidence; no longer comparing ourselves or our circumstances to others. Theodore Roosevelt said, "Comparison is the thief of joy."

Finally, we must **develop a grateful heart**. Gratefulness is a choice. I used to think that in order to be grateful, good things had to be happening in my life. I definitely didn't feel like saying, "Thank you," for the messes in my life! I had adopted the world's way of thinking: If everything was going well in my life and I was happy, then I'd be grateful. There's absolutely nothing wrong with wanting nice things or wanting good things to happen in our lives. It only becomes wrong if we are using external things to create happiness and produce gratitude.

A grateful heart must be developed on purpose and is not based on circumstances. I have learned that a grateful heart has nothing to do with my feelings, but everything to do with God's freedom in my life. As God's truth transformed my thinking, I began to experience freedom in the area of comparison and jealousy. I made a decision to place my focus on what *I did have* rather than focusing on what *I didn't have*. I chose to be thankful *on purpose*. I was able to see what God had given me and remind myself that God had a plan and a purpose for me.

We are all on our own journey. Although we are running the same race, each of our stories is unique. God hasn't forgotten about you. He has great things in store for your life. Allow God to show you who you are in Him. Embrace the real you and begin walking in the freedom that Christ died to give you. Don't allow the enemy to derail you from your destiny. Be proud of who you are—you are a masterpiece!

LISTENING TO THE VOICE OF GOD:

1. Ask God to reveal to you a gift He's placed in you that makes you unique.

2. Take time this week to write a letter or prayer to God. Start by telling God your struggles in the area of jealousy. Ask Him to reveal any lies you have believed that have led to your struggle with comparison and jealousy. Ask Him to show you the truth about your beliefs. Be honest with God; He already knows your heart and loves you. Allow Him to bring to your remembrance any event that may have opened the door for the enemy to gain access into your life.

TODAY'S DECLARATION:

I will thank God for who He created me to be. I will be happy for others when they are blessed, and remember that God has great things in store for me.

DAY 4

WALLS—TEARING DOWN WALLS FROM YOUR PAST

It is for freedom that Christ has set us free. Stand firm, then, and do not let yourself be burdened again by a yoke of slavery, **Galatians 5:1.**

What do you do when the past won't stay in the past; when the past is attacking your present; and when the past has convinced you, *this is just who you are?*

Have you ever made a mess or mistake so big you wondered how you could ever be forgiven? You might even be thinking that God could never forgive this sin—it's way too big! Maybe you weren't the one that made the mistake. Possibly someone else committed the offense against you. If you're sitting in a place of confusion, wondering how you will ever be able to let go of the past and walk in freedom, then keep reading—this is for you.

We have all made mistakes. The truth is, "for all have sinned and fallen short of the glory of God," **Romans 3:23**. There may be events from your past that leave unwanted memories, reminding you of your pain. The events in your past might be mistakes you've made or could come from another person's bad choices. Regardless of where the mistakes originated, the pain those mistakes bring has a direct impact on your life.

Satan takes great pleasure in using the pain from our past to keep us stuck in the past—which keeps us from enjoying the abundant life Jesus died to give us. Have you ever experienced an event in your life and no matter how hard you tried to forget; the memory clung to you like an unwanted companion? Every day we have an "unwanted companion" who roams around looking for someone to devour. He preys on the vulnerable. Daily he whispers in your ear, reminding you of what you've done or the injustice that was done to you by another. What do you do when the voice of the enemy becomes too loud to ignore? What happens when you've reached a point of hopelessness, convinced that this is how it will always be; it's just who you are?

I have spent many days, months, and years reliving events of my past. Maybe you're like me, and you too wonder if there will ever be a day where you don't re-live your past. I want you to know that God is a God of redemption, reconciliation, and restoration. He knew what you would do before you made the choices that brought you to where you are today. He is the God Who will redeem you by taking your mess (if you allow Him) and giving you a message about His goodness. It is impossible to out-sin God! He knows the beginning from the end. You and your mistakes were no surprise to Him.

There were certain events in my life that I considered part of life that had to be walked through—then there were those few areas in my life I found myself begging and pleading with God to change. Have you ever experienced pain so deep that you convinced yourself that God's arm was too short to reach that far down to lift you out? I can remember it like it was just yesterday.

That one phone call that made my heart sink and my knees buckle.

The call was from the county jail, and on the other end of the phone was a family member. He'd been pulled over for drinking and driving, but the shock that came later that day was the fact that he'd crashed into a telephone pole hard enough to cause a fatality. Miraculously (and by the grace of God) he walked away without a scratch. I'd never experienced anything like this, and up until then I suppose I lived in a bubble. I had no idea the fear that would ensue as I navigated uncharted territory—retrieving my family member from a jail cell. For lack of better terms, my world was rocked!

The phone call that I thought would destroy me, turned out to be the phone call that brought the biggest miracle. *But before I would ever see the miracle, I had to see the mess.* It was in the mess that God began to answer a question that would be pivotal to my healing. When we are met with unfortunate circumstances most of us will always ask the question, "Why?" **Why** did this happen to me? **Why** didn't God stop this from happening? When we allow God to answer our questions, transformation and restoration are the results. God's perspective allows us to the see the purpose in our pain. The truth of God's Word has healing power that exposes the lies the enemy wants us to believe and replaces them with a never-changing truth that sets us free.

It's completely normal to want to understand why something happened. The problem arises when we allow the wrong source to answer our questions. You've probably read the verse, "The thief comes only to steal, kill, and destroy, but I came to give you life to the fullest or in abundance," **John 10:10**. In this verse, we see two sources available to provide the answer to our questions—God or the thief (Satan). Of course, God is the most reliable and trustworthy source. God is the source of truth that brings freedom and an abundant life, while the other source (Satan) brings condemnation, guilt, and shame. Satan loves when a moment-of-crisis occurs in the life of a believer. This is often when Satan gains entry into your life, telling you all the "false" reasons *why* an event took place in your life.

Satan is described in the Bible as "the Father of lies" and "in him, no truth is found,"(**John 8:44**). If you know that Satan cannot tell the truth about your circumstances or who you are, why do you spend so much time listening to and agreeing with the lies? The answer can be found in **2 Corinthians, Chapter 10**. There is a war going on, in which you are instructed to stand and fight. Paul describes it as a *spiritual battle*. All spiritual battles start in your mind and if not recognized, can spill out into other areas of your life also.

"The weapons we fight with are not the weapons of the world. On the contrary, they have divine power to demolish strongholds," **2 Corinthians 10:4.** A *stronghold* is a place (in your mind or heart) where a particular belief is strongly upheld. I like to say it this way: a stronghold is a pattern of negative thinking that disagrees or contradicts the Word of God that you hold in your heart.

When something or someone wounds you, you have a choice.

You must decide who will you allow to answer the question of, *"why?"* If you allow the enemy to answer this question, you will most certainly receive a lie as the answer. This lie becomes the foundation by which you then begin to tailor your life. That lie becomes woven into *your reality.* You begin to live the lie as if it were the truth. The lie often forces you to believe that you must protect yourself. We protect ourselves by creating barriers or walls that keep others from getting too close. Because after all, the enemy has convinced us that, "if they knew what I've done or who I really am...."

Think about the walls in your home. Each wall separates one room from another. If you want to be alone in your home, you simply walk into a room and close the door. By closing the door, you are separated from others in the house. Just like the walls in your home, you can build walls in your heart. Walls that separate you from God and from who you really are in Christ. When you close the door to the truth, walls are formed, strongholds are built. When you believe and agree with the lies the enemy offers about your identity, your circumstances, or others in your life, you no longer walk in God's truth. *The more you replay the lies in your mind the deeper the lie becomes rooted in your heart, thus creating a stronghold.*

Are there walls in your life that are keeping you from knowing and experiencing the truth about your past—about who God says you are? The Bible says, "you will know the truth and the truth will set you free," **John 8:32**. The truth will tear down the walls of your past. It is this divine power of truth that Paul speaks of in **2 Corinthians, Chapter 10** that tears down the strongholds in your life. God's Word is the only weapon that will demolish the lies of the enemy and tear down the strongholds in our lives. God's truth will transform your thinking in a way that will allow you to begin seeing yourself as God sees you.

You have been set free from your past. You have been forgiven of every sin (past, present and future). The Bible says in **Isaiah 61:1**, *He came to mend broken hearts and set the captives free.* What are you holding onto from your past that is keeping you from moving forward and walking in freedom? What lies about your past have you allowed to hold you hostage?

What if, today, you gave God the lies you've been holding onto and allowed Him to replace those lies with absolute truth? It's time to take back the territory the enemy has invaded with his lies and deception—and it's time to let God reveal to you absolute truth that will bring healing and restoration to your soul.

Your past is never to remind you of your mistakes; it's always to remind you of God's miracles!

LISTENING TO THE VOICE OF GOD:

1. Ask God if there is an event from your past He wants to speak to you about. Write down anything that God brings to your mind.

2. Is there a lie you have believed about yourself because of that particular event? Ask God to show you the truth about the event. Record what God reveals to you.

3. Now that the lies have been exposed and replaced with the truth, take the time to say a prayer and tear down those walls the enemy has built, breaking the strongholds that have kept you from living a life of freedom!

   Dear Lord, thank You that You care about everything that concerns me. Your Word promises that when we seek You with all our heart, we will find You. I ask You to forgive me for anything I've allowed in my life that didn't honor You. By the authority of Your Word and in the name of Jesus I break any agreements that I have made with the enemy and I come into agreement with God's truth. I tear down every stronghold in the name of Jesus! Thank You, Jesus, for loving and setting me free. In Jesus name, Amen!

With truth, lies are exposed; and without lies, the wall cannot stand!

TODAY'S DECLARATION:

I will let go of my past and remember that I am a new creation in Christ; forgiven and set free!

DAY 5

DO'S AND DON'TS—
I'M SO CONFUSED!

Religion that God our Father accepts as pure and faultless is this: to look after orphans and widows in their distress and to keep oneself from being polluted by the world, James 1:27.

I grew up in what I'd like to think was an average "normal" home. I had a mom and a dad, a sister, and a couple of dogs. Oh, and a few parakeets that I begged my mom to buy—which all seemed to have one thing in common—*death*. I would leave the house with them alive and well—sitting upright on their perch, only to return later to see them hanging upside down—dead! Now I ask you, does a home get any more normal than that?

My family went to church regularly. And by regularly, I mean every Sunday morning, every Sunday night and every Wednesday night. I never enjoyed going to church; most days it was a dreaded occasion for me. I very distinctly remember my mom always smiling as she entered the doors of the church, greeting anyone that passed by; and I remember my dad avoiding most everyone, managing a half-grin here and there, as he made his way to his seat.

There was one particular memory from those days that is etched in my mind—starting and ending just like every other Sunday morning. We'd taken our seats in the same spot we sat in most every Sunday, then the cue was given from the man in the pulpit, "please stand, take out your hymnals and turn to page number..." There were no musical instruments, just a bunch of people singing in whatever note they thought blended—and without fail, one precious lady with hair as white as snow, singing so off-key it'd raise the ear of any dog!

Next, there was "the phrase" heard *every* Sunday morning, which came from an old gentleman in a gray suit, and was repeated on this particular morning, "This is the day the Lord has made, I will rejoice and be glad in it." With his Bible in hand, he spoke the words as if he were giving a eulogy at a funeral. Silence filled the room, his face expressionless. I remember thinking to myself that day, "He sure doesn't look like he's excited about *the day the Lord had made*. If that's rejoicing, I'd hate to see what grieving looks like!"

As the years ticked by, I continued going through the motions.

I attended church, tried hard to make right choices, and always put on my game-face around other "super" Christians. Oh, how that kind of Christianity can wear a person out! I was miserable; I didn't enjoy life and I sure *didn't* enjoy spending time with God. Come to think of it, I didn't spend any time with God. Looking back, I can see that all those years of *faking* it had been brought about by a faulty belief system. One that had been introduced to me during those Sunday mornings sitting in church watching what I thought was real Christianity. Etched into my mind was the image of a boring, very serious, no-nonsense God. I believed God was a very serious Being, Who meant business!

I had been holding an image in my heart of a very distant God; One who kept a list of my mistakes and was ready to punish me for them. It's no wonder I wasn't desperate to spend time with or get to know this God Who I thought was just waiting for me to mess up. I thought, *If God is so perfect, how could He love someone as imperfect as me?* I knew I could never measure up to what "I believed" God wanted from me. What I didn't understand was how I had developed such a distorted view of God. Was my opinion of God based on all those dreaded Sunday mornings? Was my view of God even accurate?

I knew what I had been told about God, but I never actually knew God.

I spent the better part of my teenage years trying to win my Dad's approval. Now, at the time, I didn't know I was "trying" to win his approval. I just knew that my Dad's approval wasn't freely given, and in order to gain it, my best performance was required.

Because of this, I had unknowingly agreed with a lie the enemy had planted in me at a very early age—*performance equals love*. As with most young people, my teenage years were filled with a rollercoaster of emotions—shifting directions with the wind. Add another teenager to the mix and you have a recipe for disaster! Yes, I had a sister. My sister was four years younger than me and the exact opposite in every way. You've heard the saying, "opposites attract", but in this case, whoever coined that phrase couldn't have been more wrong. My sister had my mother's personality; kind, caring and a lot less vocal than me. I had a very commanding personality, and as luck would have it, I think I inherited a little of that from my Dad. *Wink*

My Dad prided himself on taking care of our family. He made sure we had everything we needed and that things around our home were always in working condition. I can look back and remember all the things he "did" for me but, I don't remember him ever saying, "I love you," or "you look pretty." My sister and I very seldom got compliments from my Dad. I can remember thinking to myself some days, *I wonder if my Dad even likes me?* I received plenty of negative attention when I made wrong choices—and began to notice the attention I received was positive when I played sports and would always warrant a "good job" or a few instructive criticisms. Through my teenage years, I began to equate *love* with *doing*.

The more I wrestled with my relationship with my dad, the thicker the plot became for the enemy to drop another lie into my heart. One that went something like this: *if you'll do good, he will love you.* The belief that had been birthed from the lie of the enemy had taken root. I bought the lie, hook, line and sinker, and I began to operate out of that thinking. I thought, *I'll be the best at whatever I do and then he'll be proud of me.* This faulty thinking pattern would lead me to jump on the *performance treadmill,* and would lead to a never-ending cycle of defeat.

As I graduated from high school and went off to college, our relationship stayed the same. There was an unspoken distance between my Dad and me that left an ache in my heart. The truth that God began to show me was this—the ache I felt came from the disconnection between my heart and my Father God's. I learned that it is impossible to cultivate the horizontal relationships in my life without first cultivating my vertical relationship with God.

Our relationship with God is the most important relationship we will ever have.

The connection we form with our Heavenly Father directly reflects on the relationship we have with others. My relationship with God allows me to see those in my life through spiritual lenses—which enables me to see the heart behind the behaviors I may experience. Oh, how different things are when God starts speaking truth to those aching places in our hearts and connecting the dots to create an accurate picture of reality. I think back on my time at home and how much time and energy I spent feeling hurt and being angry.

Instead of looking to God for my validation, I was looking

to my Dad. God is the only One Who can fill you and empower you to live a life of freedom. Your identity and security *must* be rooted in Christ. If who you are is rooted in anything other than Jesus Christ, you are standing on shaky ground and will not withstand the storms of life. As the truth began to wash over me, my eyes were opened to see that all of us long to be loved and accepted. We were created for relationship, first with God, and then with others.

As I began to seek God, I came to understand that how I view my Earthly father is how I will view my Heavenly Father. In my life, a *performance pattern* was developed from the lie, *In order to be loved and accepted you need to be good.* This lie created a faulty belief system—one by which all relationships in my life would become patterned. Because I viewed my Dad as distant and hard to please, I began to believe God was a distant, performance-driven, perfection-seeking God. Years of seeking my father's approval would set me up for the false belief that my Heavenly Father would expect nothing less than *perfection*.

Today, I have a great relationship with my Dad.

God has shown my Dad and me the *absolute truth* that has totally transformed our relationship. I was able to recognize the lie I had allowed to take root in my heart. My performance mentality held me hostage for years and contributed to a faulty belief system that kept me from acknowledging the truth of my circumstances. My lack of understanding led me to believe that my Dad was responsible for the condition of my heart. The lies of the enemy may have held me captive for years, but thank God that He is faithful—and loves us enough to reveal the transforming truth of His Word when we cry out to Him.

So the question remains—if making all the right choices and performing perfectly isn't what God wants, then what does God want from us?

How do you view God? Do you see Him as a loving, compassionate God—One Who deeply cares about you and wants the best for you? Or do you see Him as a distant, uncaring God—One Who is waiting for you to get it all together before He can love you? Are you allowing God to be your source of acceptance, love and validation or do you look to others in your life for validation?

How you view God has a direct effect on how you respond to Him. God's primary desire is to conform you into the image of His dear Son. What God wants most from all His children is their heart. He wants to be the One you run to for your acceptance and security. **You don't have to work to earn God's love and approval—it's free of charge!** He has an agape love for you and me. It's a love that never changes. "And I pray that you, being rooted and established in love, may have power, together with all the saints, to grasp how wide and long and high and deep is the love of Christ, and to know this love that surpasses knowledge-that you may be filled to the measure of all the fullness of God," **Ephesians 3:17-19.**

Your belief systems are developed by the experiences in your life. How you view your parents plays a huge part in how you view God. The enemy uses the unfortunate things in your life to set you up for a life of misery. But there's good news, God is still on the throne and has the power to expose and expel any lies the enemy would use to derail your faith.

Faulty belief systems are sabotaging your faith and distorting the truth of God's Word.

LISTENING TO THE VOICE OF GOD:

1. Ask God to show you a lie that you have believed about Him.

2. Has the lie(s) that you have believed about God created a false belief that the enemy is using to destroy other relationships in your life?

3. Ask God to give you five words that describe His character and nature.

4. Ask God to show you what relationship in your life that He would like to restore. When He shows you the relationship, ask Him what you need to do to take the first step, by faith, to begin to renew your thinking toward this person.

Don't allow one more lie of the enemy to derail you from experiencing all that God has for you. God is compassionate, His ways are just and His mercies are new every morning. There is nothing that can separate you from the love of God. God's Word is TRUE, POWERFUL, AND TRANSFORMING. No matter what you see around you, no matter what you've experienced in your past, God is good all the time! He promises to work everything out for the good of those who love Him. His faithfulness will shine brightly in your life as you rest in the truth of His Word.

TODAY'S DECLARATION:

I believe God is a compassionate and loving Father. His love for me is unconditional and is not based on my performance—I am loved because I am His child.

DAY 6

GOD, IS THAT YOU? — PLUGGING
INTO THE ULTIMATE POWER SOURCE

We learned in the previous chapter that our identity in Christ is determined by who God says we are. In order for us to truly know who we are and to begin walking in that confidence, we must hear from the One who created us. There's nothing more empowering than *knowing* the voice of God.

It was an ordinary day for a guy named Moses. While in the midst of his daily task of tending sheep, he noticed a bush that was on fire—yet it was not burning up! Moses moved closer to investigate and got the surprise of his life. "When the Lord saw that he had gone over to look, God called to him from within the bush, "Moses! Moses!" (**Exodus 3:2-4**). Suddenly, the voice of God called out to Moses from the burning bush. I don't know about you, but a voice coming from a bush that knew my name would give me cause to vacate the premises! Instead of running away, the Bible says Moses moved closer—to gain a better perspective and to hear the voice of God.

Samuel, a young boy with little knowledge of God, was another one the Lord spoke to. Samuel's mother, Hannah, was barren. She prayed for a child and promised God that if He would bless her with a son, she would dedicate him to the Lord. "And she made a vow saying, "O Lord Almighty, if you will only look upon your servant's misery and remember me and not forget your servant but give her a son, then I will give him to the Lord for all the days of his life," **1 Samuel 1:11**. The Lord answered her prayer and blessed Hannah with a son, whom she named Samuel.

Because of his mother's vow, after he was weaned Samuel grew up in the house of Eli, a priest of the Lord. One night as Samuel slept he heard someone call his name. Thinking that it was Eli calling, he ran to him and replied, "Here I am, for you called me." But Eli had not called his name. Three times the Bible says that the Lord called to Samuel and on the third time, Eli realized it was the voice of God that Samuel was hearing. What I find most interesting and exciting is that God still chose to speak to Samuel even though he wasn't familiar with the Word of the Lord. "Now Samuel did not yet know the Lord: The word of the Lord had not yet been revealed to him," **1 Samuel 3:7**.

I wonder how many times we miss the Lord's leading because we have not yet learned to recognize His voice? When I was younger, I use to think it was a little creepy whenever I heard someone say, "The Lord told me," or "the Holy Spirit showed me." I remember thinking, "Are they guests in your house?" "Did you have lunch with them?" But what I really thought, and hate to admit was, "You're weird!"

My reaction was to think that *God speaking* was strange—because I hadn't yet learned the truth about God speaking to His children. I honestly thought that if you were *super spiritual* then you might be qualified to hear from God. I wasn't exactly sure what *super spiritual* meant, but I knew I wasn't included in that group! The sad reality is there are many Christians who love God, but either they don't know God still speaks to us, or they don't believe He would speak to them. We know that God spoke in the Old Testament, but does He still speak today? If He does speak to us, how do we learn to recognize His voice?

It is common to think that when we talk about *hearing* something, we are referring to an audible sound. So, it makes perfect sense to think that *hearing* God is referring to an audible voice. There are many ways that God speaks to His children, but before we go any further, I want to clarify a question you might already be pondering, "Does God speak in an audible voice?"

There are three words used to describe God that I think will help answer this question: **Omnipresence**—God is everywhere, **Omnipotence**—God is all powerful, and **Omniscience**—God is all knowing. These three words are extremely important for us to understand when we want to know Who God is and how He communicates with us.

God is everywhere—the past, the present, and the future.

God is all-powerful—*He can do what He chooses to do, however He chooses to do it.* His omnipotence includes how He chooses to speak to His children. God can—if He chooses—speak to us through an audible voice. However, most of the time He speaks to our heart, as our spirit is connected to His spirit. Finally, God is all-knowing—*He not only knows everything we need, He knows what we need to hear and how we need to hear it.*

Let's take a look at the different ways God speaks to us today:

1. **The Bible** is a great place to start hearing God. **God speaks to us through scripture. 2 Timothy 3:16** states, "all scripture is God-breathed and is useful for teaching, rebuking, correcting and training in righteousness."

2. **Prayer** is a powerful way to hear God speak. Prayer is simply a conversation with God that allows us to speak with Him and hear Him daily. Prayer increases our awareness of God's presence. Prayer builds our faith and opens the door for God to work in our lives.

3. **Dreams and Visions** are another way God can speak to us. "In the last days, God says, I will pour out my spirit on all people. Your sons and daughters will prophesy, your young men will see visions, your old men will dream dreams," **Acts 2:17**. It is important to note that the difference between *a dream and a vision is that a dream is given when a person is asleep and a vi-*

sion is given when a person is awake. God spoke to people many times using visions. Examples are Joseph, son of Jacob; Joseph, the husband of Mary; Solomon; Isaiah; Ezekiel; Daniel; Peter and Paul.

4. **Impressions** are another way God likes to speak to us. Was there ever a time when you felt led to do something for someone? That was an impression. An impression is a feeling that we get that moves us to do things that we might not do if not led by the Holy Spirit.

5. **Words of Prophecy** is a great way to hear from God. Prophecy is simply a word from God given to encourage someone. The Bible says, "everyone who prophesies speaks to men for their strengthening, encouragement, and comfort," **1 Corinthians 14:3**. A true word of prophecy is never meant to frighten or discourage you. When it's from God, it will always agree with His Word!

If you're feeling skeptical about hearing from God, please know that you're not alone. I clearly remember the first time I experienced hearing the voice of God. I was in my thirties and not very disciplined about spending time with God or listening for His voice—but that all changed the day I actually *did* hear His voice. That day, in my quiet time with God, I clearly heard Him call my name. He began to speak into my life about the plans He had for my future. There was an indescribable power that came with the

Words I received, and I knew without a doubt that I had indeed heard His voice.

One of the most common questions that we, as Christians, have when listening for God's voice is, "How do I know if I am just hearing my own thoughts, or if it is really God's voice?

For God speaks again and again, though people do not recognize it, **Job 33:14** (NLT).

It's important that we know how to recognize the voice of God. One of the best ways to get to know someone is to spend time with that person—and the same is true about God. If we want to know God, we must spend time with God. The more time we spend with Him, the more we learn about His character and His nature. Knowing someone intimately helps us discern their voice. The same is true of God; the more time we spend with God, the better we can discern His voice.

Here are a couple of questions I found helpful as I was learning to recognize God's voice: *Does what I'm hearing agree with God's Word? Does what I'm hearing agree with God's character and God's nature?*

There's a great description of God's character identified in **Galatians 5:22-23**, "But the fruit of the spirit is **love, joy, peace, patience, kindness, goodness, gentleness, faithfulness**, and **self-control**." When I'm praying and I feel like the Lord is saying something specific to me, I like to use this verse as a guideline. Is what I'm hearing filled with love, does it bring me joy, and does it bring a calmness to my heart in the area that I'm praying about? If what I'm hearing does not line up with what God would say about me or my circumstance, then I know for certain I'm hearing from the enemy—which brings me the opposite of God's nature (fear, sadness, confusion, guilt, selfishness, anger). We can always trust God's Word and His way!

I want you to pause for a moment and become completely still. As you sit quietly, close your eyes and begin making a mental note of any noises you hear around you. What did you hear? The noises you heard became obvious to you the moment you became *aware* of them.

In order to hear God, we must become aware of His presence.

I remember the first time I heard the voice of God. It was something I'd never heard before, yet seemed oddly familiar. *Could that really be God speaking to me*, I wondered? As I sat quietly pondering whether or not it was the voice of God, I had this overwhelming peace wash over me. There are no words to explain the experience, except to say, GOD. When you hear the voice of God, the Spirit inside you will confirm with your spirit that it is indeed Him.

"The Spirit himself testifies with our spirit that we are God's children," **Romans 8:16**; "He who belongs to God hears what God says," **John 8:47**; "Call to me and I will answer you, and will tell you great and hidden things that you have not known," **Jeremiah 33:3**.

Awareness of God's presence positions you to hear His voice. If you're ready to hear God, start by asking Him a few questions. God is concerned about everything in our lives, big and small. Below are questions that will get you started on your journey toward hearing God.

Write down anything God speaks to you as you ask Him these simple questions. Take time to listen after each question and allow God to answer you. One thing you should know; the enemy can't stand it when we spend time with God. Satan knows how powerful God's words are, and he will use everything he can to try and distract you from hearing the voice of God. I've written a simple prayer that I think will help you enter into God's presence and prepare your heart to hear from Him.

Dear Lord, I'm thankful that You hear me. Your Word says that if I call on You, You will answer me. Please teach me how to sit in Your presence and hear Your voice.

LISTENING TO THE VOICE OF GOD:

1. God, do You like me?

2. God, do you love me?

3. God, do you think about me every day?

4. God, what's your favorite pair of shoes that I wear?

5. God, what if you and I were going to take a trip together, where would we go and why?

6. God is there a lie that I've believed about myself?

7. God, would you tell me what makes me unique?

8. God, what do I do that makes you smile?

9. God, is there someone in my life that I need to talk to you about?

10. God, would you show me if there's anything in my heart that I'm struggling with that you want me to give to you today?

God's greatest desire is for His children to spend time with Him. It's during this time that we are able to lay aside the day's demands and simply sit with God allowing Him to love on us. God knows that life can be burdensome. We were not designed to carry the load on our own. I want to challenge you to spend time with God daily. Ask the Lord to show you *who He is* and *who He says you are*. One Word from God has the power to change a lifetime of heartache. Will you allow God access to the most vulnerable place in your heart? Let God speak words of life over you and be amazed at the transforming power of God's love!

TODAY'S DECLARATION:

I will become aware of God's presence and remember that He is always speaking to me.

DAY 7

THE FINISH LINE—
HOW LONG UNTIL WE'RE THERE?

Let your eyes look straight ahead; fix your gaze directly before you, **Proverbs 4:25.**

Have you ever attempted to do something, but after starting you wondered why you ever thought it was a good idea in the first place? I had that exact experience not too long ago. I love to run and the thought of achieving a new distance excites me! Some would call my eagerness *motivating*, but most (my family included) would call it crazy! One of my favorite places to run is at my parent's house in the country. I love to run on those back roads where the trees are full of changing colors, and the terrain is anything but flat. This one particular day stands out in my mind because this was *the run I thought would never end.*

I had set out on a route that I'd taken several times before, but this time, I had this wild idea to take a turn that I'd never taken. After 6 miles of enjoying the scenery, I approached what appeared to be Mount Everest! Of course, I'm in Texas, so it wasn't covered with snow, but it was anything but flat. As I approached the hill I began the self-motivating talk—you know how it goes, "Come on, you can do this," "It's not that bad," "Just keep going. You'll be at the top in no time." Then the other voice that can be all-too-familiar began to override the self-motivating one, "Are you crazy, you'll never make it up that thing!" "Why don't you just turn around and go back the way you came, or better yet, QUIT!" But then, just as I was about half-way up the hill, my heart pounding out of my chest, the Lord said something to me that drowned out all the other options, **"Keep your eyes on where you're going."**

The Apostle Paul used these words to define the Christian walk, "So we fix our eyes not on what is seen, but on what is unseen. For what is seen is temporary, but what is unseen is eternal," **2 Corinthians 4:18.** Keeping your eyes on where you are going reminds you that *where you are isn't your final destination.* How often have you gotten overwhelmed by the circumstances in your life? You become overwhelmed because you've taken your eyes off God and placed it on your problems.

Maintaining your focus on God is the key to walking in victory.

Are you struggling to understand the road you've been called to walk? Do events in your life, or that of those around you, make you begin to question the God you serve? If you answered yes, you are not alone. We won't always know *the why* to the things we endure, but we will always know the *Who*—the One Who promises to walk with us every step of the way. He promises to *never leave you or forsake you.* He promises when the storms of life rage, the water will not sweep you away. And, the best promise of all, *He is coming back and will make all things right.*

> *He who was seated on the throne said, "I am making everything new!" Then he said, "Write this down, for these words are trustworthy and true,"* **Revelation 21:5.**

How do we keep our eyes fixed on Jesus when life doesn't go as planned? How do we stay focused on God's Kingdom when our world gets turned upside-down? What do we do when opposition stares us in the face? How do we maintain our walk of faith when evil appears to be winning the race?

I want to tell you about a man known as one of the greatest Apostles of his time. His name is Paul. If anyone can relate to a life of suffering this man can. What I find most incomprehensible about Paul is his faithfulness to continue speaking the truth despite the suffering he endured. In case you don't know much about Paul, let me introduce you. Paul didn't start out as a representative of Christ—in fact, he was just the opposite. Paul, originally known as Saul, was a man who zealously persecuted the Christian Church. Paul later became one of God's greatest chosen instruments—a man who would be used to proclaim the Gospel. But, first, there was a God-ordained encounter with Jesus that had to happen.

The story is found in **Acts 9:1-19**, and takes place on the road to Damascus. As he was traveling to Damascus to persecute the Christians, Saul encountered a bright light—one so blinding that it caused him to fall to the ground. The Bible says that he was blind for three days; and on the third day, the Lord sent a man named, Ananias, to place his hands on him to restore his sight. This encounter with the Lord was so great that it transformed him from the inside-out.

God had chosen Paul to go out and preach the Gospel of Jesus Christ—the very One he had been persecuting. Along the way, Paul endured strong opposition and adversity that caused him great suffering. The strength and perseverance of Paul reminds me of a movie that I stumbled upon one day. I'm sure you've heard of the movie, *Rocky*. This particular movie was the one where Rocky decides that he's going to take on the biggest challenge of his career. Against the advice of family and friends, he heads off to Russia to begin the most intense physical and mental training of his life. Upon arriving in Russia, he is whisked away to a remote cabin in the middle-of-nowhere. Do you know the scene I'm talking about? There's nothing in sight as he steps out of the car, and what he does next shows his determination—despite all the obstacles. It's cold, it's snowing and there are no visible roads, but Rocky begins to run despite the pain—all with the end result in mind. He goes into strict training, knowing he has a tough job ahead of him. He doesn't let the opposition take him out; he pushes back. I guess you know that in the end he's victorious. He defeats the biggest, tallest and strongest Russian there ever was!

Now, I'm not saying Paul is *Rocky*, but I am saying that if you want to endure the race before you, you must move forward with the end in mind. You must know in advance that the road ahead will be marked by adversity. The Bible says in **John 16:33**, that we will have trouble. The trouble you experience is often a scheme of the enemy to take you out of the game; to force you to quit the race before you reach the finish line.

During the First Century, the Romans began celebrating the Olympic Games. If you follow the Olympics today, you know that the competitors go into strict physical training for months, and even years, before competing. Knowing that the early Christians were familiar with these events, Paul would use the Olympic Games as an analogy for the believers' life of faithfulness. As you read the words of Paul throughout the New Testament, there is a common theme—*perseverance*. He encourages the people to *stay the course*, to *fight the good fight of faith* and keep going regardless of what they see in front of them.

Paul learned, that through Jesus, he had the strength and power to continue his journey. I long to have the faith and perseverance of Paul! I pray that my faith-walk will be an inspiration to those around me. It is often through our struggles that we encounter God's strength and the power to continue our journey. The greatest witness we have as Christians is allowing others to see His strength and power in our lives as we walk out our faith during times of intense trial. *It's in His strength that our greatest victories are won!*

We do this by keeping our eyes on Jesus, the champion who initiates and perfects our faith. Because of the joy awaiting him, he endured the cross, disregarding its shame. Now he is seated in the place of honor beside God's throne, **Hebrews 12:2** (NLT).

Here's what I know—My God can move mountains; My God can part the Red Sea in my life; My God can walk on water; My God can give me peace when the waves are raging in the storm; My God knows the beginning from the end, and *My God Knows Me!* This same powerful God knows you, too! God knows you intimately. He knows your heart's greatest hurts, and He knows your deepest desires. Your race has been set and the course has been marked—and, the best part is that when your race is over, you will be seated at the right hand of the Father.

It's time to throw off those things that have entangled you—the worries, the hurts, and the disappointment—all the things that haven't gone as you'd expected or longed for. Start running your race with purpose—knowing and believing that God is waiting at the finish line to embrace you with arms-wide-open. When you cross that finish line you will hear the words of a loving Father say, "Well done, my good and faithful servant. Welcome home!"

No matter what lies ahead of you, know that without a doubt your God has already gone before you, and He is cheering you on to the finish-line!

LISTENING TO THE VOICE OF GOD:

1. Why do you think Paul was able to continue his walk with God despite all the suffering he endured?

2. Has an event occurred in your life that challenged everything you knew to be true about God? How did you respond? Ask God to show you the truth about your experience, and write down what He shows you.

3. Knowing that God has already provided all you need to run your race with perseverance—and that at the end of your race you'll be victorious—how does it change the way you view your circumstances? Does it change how you will run your race?

TODAY'S DECLARATION:

I will run my race with perseverance remembering that I am victorious because God is my coach.

DAY 8

FORGIVENESS—DO I HAVE TO?

Be kind hearted to one another, tenderhearted, forgiving one an-other as God in Christ forgave you, **Ephesians 4:32.**

There was a time in my life when I was faced with the choice to forgive a person who broke my heart and betrayed my trust. *How could I forgive someone who willingly hurt me, not once, but several times? What would happen if I chose to forgive them? Would they see my forgiveness as permission to hurt me again?* I tried many times to do what "I thought" was forgiving this person. I tried ignoring the situation and ignoring the person—but in doing that, the hurt only grew.

Bitterness, resentment, and anger took up permanent residence in my heart. I had emotionally shut down and wanted no part of this thing called *forgiveness*. I knew in my heart what God was calling me to do, but everything in me was having a fit. Have you ever witnessed a small child throwing a temper tantrum in the store because they were told to put the toy back on the shelf? That was the scene playing out in my heart! There was a wrestling match going on between God and me—and the anger that had wrapped itself around my heart so tightly was choking the life out of me. Forgiving this person seemed out of the question and to be honest, impossible! As I kept wrestling with God, rehearsing all the reasons I shouldn't have to forgive or couldn't forgive, God dropped this little but *powerful* thought into my heart, "I forgave you."

Stop and let that truth sink in, "God forgave you." *Even while you and I were still sinners Christ died for us,* (**Romans 5:8**). Jesus' finished work on the cross provides not only forgiveness of *all* our sins but a direct connection to the Father. It's this connection with Him that provides us with the grace and the power to forgive those that have wounded us. Let's be honest, there are some wounds that have left gaping holes in our hearts and letting go seems unfathomable! What do you do when faced with the need to forgive, but everything in your heart is screaming, *No! I Won't! I Can't!*

Forgiveness is not letting the person that offended or hurt you off the hook; it's taking them off your hook and placing them in God's hands. The person is still accountable for their actions, just not by you. We can look at forgiveness as giving God back His right to fairly judge the injustice done to us. "Dear friends, never take revenge. Leave that to the righteous anger of God. For the Scriptures say, "I will take revenge; I will pay them back," says the LORD," **Romans 12:19** (NLT).

How many times must I forgive those who hurt me?

One day, as the disciples were walking together, a conversation arose about *forgiveness*. I can only assume—based on the topic of conversation—that like you and me, Jesus' disciples had the same struggles we do concerning matters of the heart. Peter asked Jesus the following question to help settle the matter, "Lord, how many times shall I forgive my brother when he sins against me? Up to seven times?" **Matthew 18:21**. Peter is one individual that I can't wait to meet when I get to heaven. He always has something to say and usually at the wrong time. Reminds me of myself at times. If you notice, after Peter asked Jesus the question, he added another question with what *he thinks* is the answer to the first one.

Can you imagine the scene? Peter is walking along with his motley crew, and they begin to talk about how many times we are to forgive someone. Of course, Peter thinks he knows the answer! With his outspoken and confident personality, he poses the question with his answer tacked on the end—*Jesus, how many times are we supposed to forgive someone who wrongs us? Seven times, right?* Jesus' answer stuns them all—and I'm sure left Peter speechless—"I tell you not seven times, but seventy-seven times." Some translations read, *up to seventy times seven*, which, if you do the math, is a whopping 490 times! That's a whole lot of forgiveness!

The lesson Jesus is teaching us isn't that you and I are to carry around a scorecard, checking a box each time we forgive someone. He is teaching that our *freedom* in Christ is directly connected to the *forgiveness* that we extend to others. There is no limit on the kind of forgiveness Jesus taught His disciples about that day. Jesus not only taught it but also demonstrated the kind of forgiveness He is calling all believers to embrace. His last day on earth, as Jesus hung on a cross for you and me, He said the words that He is asking us to repeat, "Please forgive them for they know not what they do," **Luke 23:34**. What could possibly allow Him to have a heart filled with that much forgiveness? He endured torture, deception, insults—yet through it all He embraced a heart of humility. *Grace, mercy, love*—the power source that flowed from God's heart to the heart of His Son hanging on that cross. Today that same power source is available to you and me!

I learned through God's truth what forgiveness was and *what it was not*. Forgiving another is not condoning their wrong choices. Forgiveness is not saying that what someone did to you is acceptable. Forgiveness is not giving another permission to mistreat you. Forgiveness is letting God handle the injustice done to you.

Forgiveness is not forgetting, it is choosing to let go of the offense.

For I will forgive their wickedness and will remember their sins no more, **Hebrew 8:12**.

How do you take the first step towards forgiveness? Step one begins with a choice. I can recall many times trying to forgive—and waiting to *feel* like forgiving—only to realize the *feeling of wanting to forgive* never appeared. God gives you and me the grace to forgive. Grace gives us the ability to do certain things we otherwise would not have the power and strength to do on our own. Forgiveness is not easy, but with God's strength, it is possible.

One of the most important lessons I learned—the hard way—was how refusing forgiveness produced a lack of freedom in my life. The longer I held on to the offense, the wider the door opened for the enemy. *Anytime we refuse to obey what God is calling us to do, we are giving the enemy permission to enter the door of our heart.*

Here are three reasons you need to forgive—and why God places so much value on your forgiveness of others:

1. *God first forgave you.* God demonstrated His love for you by taking your place on the cross. God sent His only Son so that you could live. God continues to display His love for you daily by giving you a fresh start each new day. The Bible says in **Lamentations 3:22, 23**, "His mercies are new every morning." God doesn't keep a record of your wrong doings; He is faithful to forgive you when you repent and ask for forgiveness. Until you grasp and believe this truth, it will be impossible for you to also forgive as Jesus did.

2. *Holding onto hurt leads to bitterness and resentment*—and will always lead to self-destruction. In reality, holding someone hostage for the wrong they've committed against you, holds *you* hostage. Chances are the person that you're holding hostage isn't even thinking about you. That may sound harsh, but the reality is, holding bitterness and resentment in your heart only punishes you, not the offender.

3. *Choosing not to extend forgiveness disconnects your heart from God's heart.* Notice I didn't say God's *love.* Many times we are led to believe that our choices determine God's love for us. The truth is, God never stops loving you—but it does break His heart when you choose your way over His will. Everything that God asks you to do is for your own good. God will never require you to do anything that He first doesn't equip you to do. When you choose to ignore the need to forgive another, your heart is pulled away from God's heart. Essentially, you disconnect from your ultimate power source when you choose to withhold forgiveness from another. Remember, it's God's strength and not your own, that allows you to forgive.

How do you know you have forgiven? Does it mean you never think about *it* anymore? Does it mean there's nothing else to do once you've made the choice to forgive? I thought I knew the answer to these very questions until the day a storm came, and scattered my thinking in a million pieces!

Something very unexpected happened to me one particular morning. Thinking I had dealt with all the emotions that came from a previously wounded heart, a situation arose that literally caused those old emotions to explode from my heart like a volcano erupting! As the emotions swirled around in my head, and I desperately tried to get myself grounded, I wondered, *where did all that come from? Hadn't I dealt with all those hurt feelings long ago? Hadn't I forgiven that person?* As I sat and surveyed the damage left in the wake of the words I had spoken, I was reminded of a verse found in **Galatians 5:1**, "It is for freedom that Christ has set us free. Stand firm, then, and do not let yourselves be burdened again by a yoke of slavery." As I wondered what this verse could possibly have to do with forgiveness, the Lord began to speak to my heart. He said, *forgiveness is a process and something that you must continue to walk in*. I had forgiven this person, but what I had neglected was the daily maintenance of my heart. Our freedom in Christ is something we must do daily.

Forgiveness is part of the freedom walk.

Walking out your freedom requires you to take a daily inventory of your heart's condition—allowing God to show you any areas of your life you are trying to manage in your own strength. The Apostle Paul was reminding us that if we do not stand firm in the truth, the enemy will remind us of the hurt that once wrapped itself around our hearts—and if not guarded, that hurt will find its way back. The lesson I learned that day was, *forgiveness isn't something we do just one time, forgiveness is a part of who we are in Christ*. We are called to extend forgiveness to others each day. **Forgiveness is an extension of Christ's love for us—extending through us towards those in our lives.**

Once you forgive another, guarding your heart and mind against the enemy is vital to maintaining victory in this area. Satan loves to use the wounds of the past to gain access into your life. The enemy knows the areas in your life that are the most vulnerable—and he will use those areas to attack your mind and emotions if you are not alert to his schemes. I had forgiven, but I had also dropped my guard. **I began to entertain thoughts from the past, instead of taking them captive to the Word of God.** The day that argument transpired with the person I had forgiven all those years back, I was unarmed, unclothed and unaware. I did not understand when I made the choice to forgive this person, with the help of the Holy Spirit, Satan also made a choice—the choice to file that transaction away, to be used at a later date in my life.

I am so grateful for the truth of God's Word. "The Word of God is alive and active. Sharper than any double-edged sword, it penetrates even to dividing soul and spirit, joints and marrow; it judges the thoughts and attitudes of the heart," **Hebrews 4:12**. The Word of God has the power to heal and transform those broken places in our hearts.

I hope this chapter has stirred something in your heart. Please understand that it is never okay for someone to mistreat or abuse another. If this has happened to you, I want you to know how sorry I am that this happened. God's heart aches when you hurt. He holds every tear that you've ever shed in the palm of His hand. "You keep track of all my sorrows. You have collected all my tears in your bottle. You have recorded each one in your book," **Psalm 56:8**.

God will take what Satan has meant for evil in your life and will turn it around for His glory!

Will you allow God to mend your broken heart? Will you give

Him access to that place in your heart that has been pierced by the actions or the words of another? Will you take the person that has been on *your hook* and place them on God's? It's time to stop allowing the enemy to keep you from the freedom that Christ died to give you. Take a step of faith and watch what God will do as you extend forgiveness to those who have hurt you. Remember, forgiving someone is not accepting or condoning their behavior. Forgiveness is not giving another permission to offend again. Forgiveness doesn't automatically mean your trust with that person is renewed. Forgiveness starts with a choice and is required daily so that you can continue walking in the freedom that Christ died to give you.

As you take a step of faith, God will meet you; He will enable you to do what you are incapable of doing on your own. Hearing the voice of God can free your heart, transform your mind and repair your relationships.

Open your heart and let God lead the way!

LISTENING TO THE VOICE OF GOD:

1. God, is there someone that I need to take off *my hook* and place in Your Hands?

2. God, is there a lie I have believed about *what forgiveness is*? Help me to understand the truth about forgiveness.

3. God, would you show me what I can do *each day* to walk in freedom in the area of forgiveness in my life?

TODAY'S DECLARATION:

Today, I choose to forgive those who have hurt me, not because I feel like it, but because I choose to do things God's way.

DAY 9

TAKE IT BACK!

What started out as a "holy" prayer quickly turned into a list of complaints. I was trying my hardest to maintain an *attitude of gratitude*, but somewhere along the way, between the words, "thank You" and "think You" my prayer took an unexpected turn. Let me explain. As I began thanking God for the blessings in my life, my mind began to wander to all my frustrations. My wording went from, "**Thank You**," to "*Do You **think You** can do these things for me?*" *God, don't You **think You** can do something to help me with the problems I'm experiencing? Don't You **think You** can fix a few people in my life? Don't You **think You** can stop all the evil going on in the world?*

As I kept scrolling through the pages in my mind of all the wrongs in my life, suddenly I was jolted back to reality as The Lord spoke these words to my heart, *Take it back!* Those three words of instruction brought my moaning to a halt. As I pondered those words, I began to ask the Lord what "**it**" was that I needed to take back. He so clearly spoke to my heart these simple words: *You are to take back the authority I've given to you.* The authority God was referring to was *His authority*—the authority that had been given to me the day He sent His son to the cross and the moment I accepted Him as my Lord and Savior.

You see, that morning as I sat praying and listing out all the things I needed God to do, I was asking God to do things that He'd already done. The enemy was defeated and disarmed, and the authority had already been handed to me. It was up to me to use the authority God had given me to stand up against the attacks of the enemy.

My neglect to use the authority given to me was feeding my frustration. It wasn't that I was not equipped to stand against the enemy; the tools I'd been given to resist him were still in my toolbox. I had been living in utter defeat and each day was just another day of turmoil and frustration. I wore my attitude of defeat like it was a badge of honor.

God never intended for us to live a life of defeat. Jesus went to the cross for our freedom. The Bible says that we are more than conquerors in Christ. We've been given authority over the power of the enemy, and in Christ, we are children of the Most High God. It's time that we live as children of the King! This kind of freedom will require confidence and boldness; but more, it will require faith. Faith is accessing what God says is rightfully yours!

You are in God's army and you must arm yourself for the battle. The war has already been won, but as long as we live in this world we will have trials. God tells us in the Book of Ephesians, we are to put on the full armor of God so that we can take our stand against the devil's schemes. So, if the war has already been won, and we are on the winning side, why do so many Christians walk around in total defeat? Could it be that we don't know what we already possess? Spiritual authority rests in *knowing who we are in Christ*. In order to take something back, we have to know what belongs to us—and we must be stronger than the one who took it.

The Bible says in **Ephesians 6:10-17**, "Be strong in the Lord and in his mighty power. **Put on *the full armor of God* so that you can take your stand against the devil's schemes.** For our struggle is not against flesh and blood, but against the rulers, against the authorities, against the powers of this dark world and against the spiritual forces of evil in the heavenly realms. Therefore put on the full armor of God, so that when the day of evil comes, you may be able to *stand your ground*, and after you have done everything, to stand. Stand firm then, with the **belt of truth** buckled round your waist, with the **breastplate of righteousness** in place, and with your feet fitted with the readiness that comes from the **gospel of peace**. In addition to all this, take up the **shield of faith**, with which you can extinguish all the flaming arrows of the evil one. Take the **helmet of salvation** and the **sword of the Spirit**, which is the word of God."

Let's look at each of these pieces of armor to get a better picture of what a warrior in God's army should look like.

Paul, who wrote this scripture, was very familiar with the soldiers of his day. Paul describes the *Christian armor* similar to that of the *Roman soldier*. He used this analogy as an example of how we are to arm ourselves for the spiritual battles we will endure.

When the Roman soldiers prepared for battle, the first piece of armor they would place around their waist was their belt. This belt was thick and wide, holding all the other pieces of armor in place, as well as protecting the vital organs in their body. The Bible says that the *first piece* of God's armor that we are to put on is called the **Belt of Truth**. This is the foundation for all of the other pieces of armor. The Belt of Truth holds us together. When we put on the Belt of Truth we are putting on Jesus; placing the truth of who God is and who we are around our waist.

The next piece of armor is the **Breastplate of Righteousness**. The Bible says that we are *the righteousness of God in Christ Jesus*. This righteousness is not due to anything that we have accomplished—it is not our own, but rather the righteousness of God. We are in right standing with God, not because we are good enough, but because of God's goodness. This breastplate *protects us* by covering the place the enemy tries to pierce and wound—*our heart*.

Next, we are to put on our **Shoes of Peace**. The Roman soldier had special sandals, designed with spikes on the bottom that would grip the ground. This allowed the soldiers to stand firm during the battle. When we, as Christians, put on the Shoes of Peace, we are standing in the peace that comes only from God. *We no longer allow what we see to change what we know.* Jesus said, "Peace I leave with you; my peace I give you. I do not give to you as the world gives. Do not let your hearts be troubled and do not be afraid," **John 14:27**. When we are going through a difficult season in life, the shoes of peace will remind us to lean on and trust in God's unfailing love.

This next piece of armor, the **Shield of Faith** is to be picked up. The soldiers used their shield as a protective covering in battle. This was no small piece of armor. The shield a soldier carried was as big as a door—enabling a soldier to hide their whole body behind it during battle. The soldiers would often place their shields end-to-end, building a wall of protection against the enemy. As a follower of Christ, Paul tells us that we are to take up our shield of faith when the enemy attacks. Satan's attacks can bring doubt in a believer's life—causing us to wonder if God will come through for us in our time of need. When we take up our Shield of Faith, we are declaring that our total trust and assurance is in God alone; and that what God has spoken is the absolute truth! The Shield of Faith, which is given to every believer, is secure and eternal. "Now faith is confidence in what we hope for and assurance about what we do not see," **Hebrews 11:1**.

After we have picked up our Shield of Faith, we are to put on the **Helmet of Salvation**. The helmet was a vital piece of armor for a soldier. The helmet protected a soldier's brain. Just as a football player would never enter a game without his helmet for fear of a head injury, we as believers should not think of entering a spiritual battle without our helmet. As Christians, our spiritual battle always starts in the mind. The mind is where the enemy attacks first. If the enemy can gain access to your mind and your way of thinking, he has gained control over your actions.

The helmet of salvation reminds us that we belong to God. When we are saved, we are given the gift of eternal life. Salvation not only promises us eternity with God, it promises us Heaven on earth *if* we operate in the Spirit. The moment you were born again you were given the gift of the Holy Spirit. The Bible says that the Holy Spirit guides you into all the truth, and is your Comforter. The Bible says that we are to, "walk in the spirit so that we do not gratify the lusts of the flesh," **Galatians 5:16**. Our spirit and our fleshly desires are in direct opposition to one another. Without the *helmet of salvation*, we are vulnerable to the enemy's attack on our mind.

The last piece of armor Paul describes is the **Sword of the Spirit**, which is the Word of God. All of the other pieces of armor are defensive in nature—used for resisting the enemy. The Sword of the Spirit is our offensive weapon, to be used against the enemy. The Bible describes the Word of God as, "alive and active," (**Hebrews 4:12**). There is power in the Word of God, and therefore, this is the only weapon that will overcome the enemy of our soul. The only way to silence the shouts of the devil is to declare out loud the truth of God's Word.

Our *spiritual authority* is exercised through our spoken word. The Bible says, "I give you all authority and power over the enemy," **Luke 10:19**. You are probably familiar with the story of David and Goliath. My favorite part of this story is found when David runs quickly to the battle line to meet Goliath face-to-face. David stood with confidence, knowing that God was with him—but, it was what he said next that gave David the strength to stand against the attack of the enemy. "You come against me with sword and spear and javelin, but I come against you in the name of the LORD Almighty, the God of the armies of Israel, whom you have defied," **1 Samuel 17:45**. David knew that the battle belonged to the Lord—and his job was to stand on the authority that God's promise and His truth provided.

It's time to start arming yourself for battle. Begin walking in the God-given authority that is rightfully yours. Start taking back the ground you have given Satan in your life. It's time to tell the devil, "No more!" No longer stand back and let Satan have his way in your life. No longer allow the enemy to hinder, block or delay the blessings of God. Choose daily to *put on the armor of God* and pick up the only offensive weapon designed to silence the enemy—the Word of God.

The battle may be raging, but the war has already been won!

I have told you these things, so that in me you may have peace. In this world you will have trouble. But take heart! I have overcome the world, John 16:33.

LISTENING TO THE VOICE OF GOD:

1. What areas in your life have you allowed the enemy access?

2. What has God provided for you that you are to "put on" in order to stand firm against the enemy?

3. Ask God how can you take back the authority that He has given you in the areas the devil has been occupying in your heart.

TODAY'S DECLARATION:

I am not fighting for victory, but rather from victory—therefore I will stand firm on the Truth of God's Word.

DAY 10

FEAR—IT'S TIME TO GO!

FEAR! It's real. It's often paralyzing—and it can suffocate your faith. Fear is one of the greatest tools the devil uses to take our focus off God. Fear brings a great deal of uncertainty and doubt about *Who God is*, or *where God is*, in our lives. If you've experienced fear, then you've more-than-likely also experienced doubt. The enemy uses fear and doubt to gain access into a believer's mind by calling into question God's goodness, and even His existence.

It started out as an ordinary day—until one phone call brought the things of that day to a screeching halt. I immediately asked myself, "How can this happen, God? Where were You, and why weren't you protecting my family?" After all, I had prayed, begged and even pleaded for God to take away the circumstances that we were now facing. I felt let down, abandoned by God; but more than that, I felt the presence of darkness like I had never felt before.

I felt enveloped in an unexplainable heaviness that made time seem to stand still.

That one phone call set in motion a series of events that would not be stoppable by human might. I became painfully aware of how vulnerable we are. I'm not speaking of just my own vulnerability, but also that of all God's children. If we are unaware of his tactics we can easily become sitting targets for the enemy of our soul. His mission is to take us out of the race and render our testimony void. What better way than to use fear as his *secret agent* of darkness.

Fear has a funny way of grabbing your attention—and before you know it, you're paralyzed—not able to take one more step of faith. It wasn't until I found myself in one of the darkest valleys I'd ever known, that I began to let the fear I was experiencing call into question the very nature of God. I doubted His goodness, and most of all I doubted His protection. I became convinced that God's faithfulness wasn't strong enough to overcome this hurdle in my life. I did not believe He could work this situation out for my good. I knew He was asking me to trust Him—no matter the outcome, but this was one declaration I couldn't muster up the courage to speak out-loud. Instead of declaring God's faithfulness, I unknowingly began to declare a lie from the enemy. The lie went something like this, "God loves me, but He won't protect me when bad things happen." The more I believed the lie, the deeper those roots grew in my heart.

Fear will either lead you to run toward God or away from God. When you feel afraid, you have a choice: You can become aware of the fear and ask God to help you or you can allow the fear to take hold and begin to control your thoughts and emotions. I must confess, I chose the latter. I allowed the fear I was experiencing to grab me by the throat—and it began to choke the life out of me. I couldn't eat, I couldn't sleep, and the anxiety I felt was unbearable. I felt completely out-of-control and looking back, I was out-of-control. But, was I ever in control? Could my *lack of control* be behind the worry, the anxiety and the gut-wrenching fear that I was experiencing? The fear was real, but what needed to become more real was *God in my circumstance.*

> ***I had no control over my present circumstance or the outcome.***

I soon realized that the only thing I had any control over was *my attitude, my emotions, and my words.* Instead of grabbing hold of God's hand, I had been grasping for ways to solve my own problem. The more I worked out of my flesh, the more I gave place to fear.

What I learned in the valley was this: God is *always* there. I couldn't see Him, but as I chose to become aware, I began to feel His presence take over the utter darkness that had loomed over my days. The Bible says in **1 John 4:18**, "There is no fear in love. Perfect love casts out (drives out) fear." I was experiencing a spirit of fear and it was time to tell this unwanted guest to get out of my house and my heart!

> ***There are two types of fear that we can experience—rational fear and irrational fear.***

Let's talk about the first type of fear: *rational fear*. This type of fear is sensible; it's a cautious fear. This is a God-given, natural emotion or response that lets us know when our safety is threatened. Rational fear can come as the result of an event that has taken place in your life—and is based on something you fear might happen again.

The second kind of fear is *irrational fear*. This type of fear is without reason or understanding. It is not based on truth or previous experience but rather based on a false belief system. This type of fear says, "I know nothing has happened, but it *could* happen." When I was younger I would spend the night at my grandmother's house. She lived in the country where street lights didn't exist. When the sun went down and the light went out, my fear went up. I was deathly afraid of sleeping by the window. When night fell, you could hear the coyotes outside singing a melody. Most times they were so loud it sounded as if there were a pack of them waiting right outside the window! Why was I so afraid? Had something happened in the past to bring about this fear? No, this type of irrational fear was based on nothing more than my wild imagination. I feared something that *could* happen—but probably never *would* happen. The enemy was not only stealing my peace, he was stealing my sleep!

I lived much of my life in a constant state of fear.

There wasn't a day that went by that I didn't think about the past, worry about the past—and dread that my past would find me in the present. My past played a huge part in my fearful thoughts. I tried praying, fasting and casting down wild imaginations, just as God commanded. No matter what I did, the fear lingered—it hovered over me like a black cloud before a storm. I was desperate for God to do something. Then, one day, He began to speak to me about what He'd already done for me. Here I was, begging for something that He had already freely given to me. The problem was, *I wasn't accessing the finished work of the cross*. The cross had already defeated anything that stood between me and complete access to Jesus. The Bible says, "He disarmed the powers and authorities, He made a public spectacle of them, triumphing over them by the cross," **Colossians 2:15**.

I was focused on the *fear*, rather than the Father. Whatever we feed begins to grow, and I was feeding my fear. Instead, I should have been smothering that fear with the truth of God's Word. God's truth is rooted in His unconditional love for His children. The enemy wanted me to believe that God's love wasn't enough to protect me. I believed that God might love me, but based on my past experience, He wouldn't protect me. The more I fed the lie, the larger it grew. When I was crumbling under the weight of my fear, I cried out to God and He began to speak truth into my heart. It is true that we live in a fallen world—sin is running wild, and the enemy is on the loose. But, here's where God turned it all around for me: He took that previous statement and stamped, *"It is finished"*, across the page. He freed me from the fear that had taken up residence in my heart and mind. I no longer had to be afraid of the enemy. God wanted me *aware* of his schemes, not *fearful* of them. I no longer had to spend my days fearing the past, the present or the future—because God had already defeated my foe! I began to understand that I would go through trials, *but* I would not be stuck in them. I would walk out victorious because God was on my side, and the victory had already been won!

The Bible repeats the phrase, *do not fear, do not be afraid, do not let your heart be troubled*, over and over again. These words were often spoken by Jesus to His disciples. These words are still true for you today. You are not to be afraid of what you see in front of you—you are to face it head-on, armed with the truth of God's Word. God's Word echoes one of His most powerful promises, "And surely I am with you always, to the very end of the age." **Matthew 28:20**. It is God's love that reminds us that, *no weapon formed against you and me will prosper*, (**Isaiah 54:17**). It is God's love that drives out fear when it comes knocking on the door of your heart. It is God's love that reminds you and me that we are His children and nothing, or no one, can snatch us out of His hand!

There are three, "**I statements**," that have helped me when fear begins to rear its ugly head in my life. I would like to share them with you:

- When I feel fear, **I recognize** my fear and where the fear is coming from, (the enemy). By recognizing the fear is not from God, I then turn my focus away from the fear and onto God. "God did not give us a spirit of fear, but one of power, love and a sound mind," **2 Timothy 1:7**.

- When I feel fear, **I remember** that God has already defeated the source of my fear. I trust God, knowing that His love for me will never fail, and He promises to protect me from all harm. "The Lord will keep you from all harm—He will watch over your life," **Psalm 121:7.**

- When I feel fear, **I recall** my identity in Christ and the authority that He has given me. "I have given you authority to trample on snakes and scorpions and to overcome all the power of the enemy; nothing will harm you," **Luke 10:19.**

The enemy is to be under our feet, not over our circumstances. It is our thoughts and beliefs that bring him to eye level. In order for Satan to remain underfoot, God must remain front and center in our lives.

Greater is he who is in me, than he who is in the world, 1 John 4:4.

LISTENING TO THE VOICE OF GOD:

1. Ask God to help you recall a time in your life when you experienced fear.

2. When you were afraid, did you find yourself running *to God* or away *from God?* Why do you think you made the choice you made at that time?

3. Ask God if there was a lie you believed in that moment of fear that you allowed to take root in your heart.

4. Ask God to reveal to you the truth about that event and the fear you experienced.

5. Ask God what He wants you to do the next time you begin to experience fear.

TODAY'S DECLARATION:

I will rest in God's love—I will not fear because God is with me.

DAY 11

SEXUAL PURITY IN A FALLEN WORLD—WHAT'S THE BIG DEAL; EVERYBODY'S DOING IT!

Then, after desire has conceived, it gives birth to sin: and sin, when it is full-grown gives birth to death, James 1:15.

Sex—it's everywhere you turn! We are inundated with sexual images designed to lure us into whatever product is on the market. Turn on the television and you'll see a commercial for a hamburger—and eating the hamburger is a tall, blonde, voluptuous woman! Certainly eating a hamburger is not sinful—it's the sexual message added to entice the viewer to *take a bite. Sex sells!*

The world is constantly sending the message, *take a bite! Take a bite of what the world has to offer you.* It's the same message the devil sent to Adam and Eve in the Garden of Eden —*take a bite and you'll be like God. Take a bite and you can have it all!* This message continues to ring loud and clear, *take a bite of what this world has to offer and you'll be powerful, rich, happy, and secure.* It's the temptation to *take a bite* of worldly pleasures that leads us to sinful actions as we choose to feed our flesh, instead of honoring God.

The Bible refers to Satan as, "the god of this world." "Satan, who is the god of this world, has blinded the minds of those who don't believe. They are unable to see the glorious light of the Good News. They don't understand this message about the glory of Christ, who is the exact likeness of God," **2 Corinthians 4:4**. The temptation that Satan offers is not only enticing the youth of this generation but the adults who are raising them, as well. Satan is luring non-believers and believers alike away from a place of security with God—to a place that will lead to utter darkness.

Immorality is running rampant in the world today.

The message of sex is everywhere you turn—billboards, television commercials, the internet, and social media. Pornography addictions, drug addictions, alcohol addictions and, yes, sex addictions are at an all time high! It all starts with a look, a drink, a snort of cocaine, the first time you have sex—followed by a quiet whisper from the enemy, "It's okay, no one will get hurt, and everybody's doing it." Addiction always starts with a *first time*. That *one moment*—set in motion by temptation—enticing you to take a step toward sin and away from God. When the sin is fully conceived in our hearts, it develops into an addiction—and we are now controlled by the enemy of our soul. "Then, after desire has conceived, it gives birth to sin: and sin, when it is full-grown gives birth to death," **James 1:15**.

Think about the one thing you treasure the most. Would you freely give that treasured item away? God did that for you. He gave His most prized possession when He sent Jesus to the cross—all so that we would be restored back into relationship with Him. Every day young children, teens, and unmarried adults are freely giving away the most prized possession that God has entrusted to them—their virginity. It's become a way of receiving attention, gaining popularity, and feeling loved.

Do you not know that your bodies are temples of the Holy Spirit, who is in you, whom you have received from God? You are not your own, **1 Corinthians 6:19**.

The lie has been set in motion that, *sex is no big deal.* The word sex has taken on a whole different meaning in our world today. Girl's clothing leaves nothing to the imagination—all because popular media says, *the shorter the better.* Debating whether or not we should provide our kids with condoms is a top story on the evening news. We all know of the young girl who hears, "I love you" for the first time and gives her virginity away. Kids are doing unspeakable things in the very schools designed to provide an education. They have been led to believe that certain acts are not considered sex, but rather a game to be won. We must understand God's heart about sexual purity and why it breaks His heart when we choose our way over His way for our lives.

God is the creator of all things—sex being one of those things.

When God created man and woman, He gave them the gift of sexual intimacy. Sex was created for a man and woman who have made a commitment to spend the rest of their lives together. Unfortunately, the enemy has taken what God designed to be enjoyed and pleasurable—and distorted it into something without value. The world is sending the message every day that, *sex is okay*—regardless of who you have it with, whether you're married or single. God specifically addresses the issue of sexual morality in His Word, so let's explore the reason God places so much value on sexual purity.

God wants the very best for His children. He has given us things on earth to enjoy, but along with those things He has placed boundaries for our protection. Sex is one of those "things" that God has set boundaries around. The Bible says, "Flee from sexual immorality. Every other sin a person commits is outside the body, but the sexually immoral person sins against his own body," **1 Corinthians 6:18**. When we choose to have sex outside of marriage we are giving away an important part of ourselves. The very act of giving yourself sexually to another was created by God to consummate the marriage covenant between a man and a woman. To consummate means to make complete. When there is sex outside of marriage, you are merely engaging in a selfish act of the flesh. You are not making anything complete, but rather the opposite happens—you make yourself incomplete by giving a piece of yourself away.

My heart's desire is that you begin to see God's heart for you—and why He holds sexual purity at such a high level of importance.

What have you done for what you thought was love? Have you allowed someone to pressure you into doing what you knew was wrong—just so you would feel loved and accepted? No matter what happened in your past, there is always forgiveness for those who call on the name of the Lord. You can start today with a clean slate. "There is no condemnation for those who are in Christ Jesus," **Romans 8:1**. It's never too late to start over in Christ.

How do you maintain sexual purity in a sex-craved world?

How do you stand against peer pressure, media overload and the temptation of the enemy? What if everything you did each day, you did it for God? What if every choice you made daily, you made for God's glory—not for the world's applause? If you allow God to direct your steps you will be able to stand your ground against the enemies schemes and glorify God in the process.

There are two forces at work each day in your mind and in your heart: the mind of Christ and the mind of the flesh. Think of it like a football game: one team is, "The Mind of Christ" and the other is, "The Mind of the Flesh." *The Mind of the Flesh* is a strong and aggressive team—one that uses intimidation tactics, and temptation as a means of controlling the game. In the offensive position is *The Mind of Christ*. This team uses the wide receiver, "Truth" to run the ball straight into the end zone—and scores the winning touchdown! When we are playing on Christ's team, we have been given truth to operate out of daily. *The Mind of Christ* is always stronger than *The Mind of the Flesh* but is up to you and me which one we will allow to fill our minds. Which team are you on? Which do you operate out of daily—*The Mind of Christ* or *The Mind of the Flesh?*

So letting your sinful nature control your mind leads to death. But letting the Spirit control your mind leads to life and peace, **Romans 8:6** (NLT).

For the flesh desires what is contrary to the Spirit, and the Spirit what is contrary to the flesh. They are in conflict with each other so that you are not to do whatever you want, **Galatians 5:17.**

God's Word speaks of *sanctification*. You might be wondering what sanctification has to do with sexual purity. Let me explain. The moment you were saved, you entered into God's family. He set you apart as His own and begins to clean you up and mold your heart to be like His. This process is known as *sanctification*. The goal of sanctification is to change something. God is changing you to become more like Him. I love the definition of sanctification—*to purify something; to make holy.* God is setting you apart for His glory. "It is God's will that you should be sanctified: that you should avoid sexual immorality; that each of you should learn to control your own body in a way that is holy and honorable, not in passionate lust like the pagans, who do not know God." **1 Thessalonians 4:3-5.**

God wants your mind to be submitted to His truth, not to the world's standards. We allow God's truth to reign in our hearts by abiding in Him. As we spend time daily in His Word and allow Him to reveal the heart behind His truth, we are forever changed. We no longer feel the need to do things to fit in or be accepted. We understand and believe that we already fit in and are accepted— by the only One Who matters. We are called, as believers, to be Spirit-led. Simply put, to be Spirit-led means to be obedient to God, believing the truth and walking out that truth in our everyday lives. **Ephesians 3:16** (AMP), tells us He enables us to be, "...strengthened and reinforced with mighty power in the inner man by the [Holy] Spirit [Himself indwelling your innermost being and personality]." It is impossible for us to be *good*, or remain sexually pure in our own strength, *but with His strength, all things are possible*, (**Mark 10:27**).

Do you not know that your bodies are temples of the Holy Spirit, who is in you, whom you have received from God? You are not your own; you were bought with a price. Therefore honor God with your bodies, **1 Corinthians 16:19-20.**

To **honor** means, to *hold in high regard*. Start today with a decision to honor God with every choice you make. Start every day by asking God to direct your steps—asking for the strength to stay sexually pure. Peer-pressure and temptation will always be a force of the enemy, used to steal something pure God has placed in you. But, as you continue to operate out of, *The Mind of the Spirit*, you will win the battle that is before you.

Don't allow the taunting of the enemy to drown out the voice of TRUTH!

LISTENING TO THE VOICE OF GOD:

1. Think back to a time in your life that you allowed the temptation and peer pressure of others to convince you to give in to sexual temptation. Ask God to show you *the truth* about the choice you made.

2. Ask God what safeguards/boundaries you can place in your life to ensure you maintain your sexual purity.

3. Ask God if there are any relationships in your life that do not bring honor to Him. Ask God what He would like you to do with those relationships.

TODAY'S DECLARATION:

I will maintain my sexual purity so that I will receive God's best for my life and glorify Him each day with my choices.

DAY 12

ANGER—3, 2, 1 BLAST OFF!

Have you ever had a complete meltdown? I mean the kind of meltdown where ugly words flew out of your mouth before you could catch them—tears flowed uncontrollably until you thought you'd pass out from lack of oxygen—and behavior so raw it left others around you speechless. If you've ever experienced what I just described then you've experienced the emotion of *anger*. Where does this anger come from and what do we do when faced with this overwhelming emotion?

Anger is a God-given emotion. The emotion of *anger* appears as a strong feeling of displeasure or irritation. I'm sure you can remember a time when you've felt a strong displeasure or irritation at someone or a particular event in your life. When I was younger I had the strange notion that anger was ungodly and definitely not an acceptable emotion for a Christian. I had a pretty nice-sized temper, and not much self-control to go along with it. As I got older, I became even more convinced that *a Christian* just didn't get angry. I'm sure you can imagine the havoc this thought wreaked in my life as I tried my best to push aside this emotion. I came to understand that although God had given me this emotion, it was up to me to decide how I would handle it.

Ephesians 4:26-27 says, "In your anger do not sin. Do not let the sun go down while you are still angry, and do not give the devil a foothold." As I read this verse, I began to understand how I was to attend to my anger. I knew I was going to get angry, but it was up to me what I did when anger showed up. The Bible clearly states, **when** you are angry, do not sin. He doesn't say **if** you are angry. God knew that we would all, at one time or another, experience anger. The next part of this verse tells me, *I'm not to hold on to anger.* "Do not let the sun go down while you are still angry." God is saying, *it is okay you're angry, but it's not okay for you to stay that way.* By choosing to hold onto offense towards another, we open the door for the enemy. The last part of this verse explains what anger will do if we allow it to take root in our hearts. It reads, "and do not give the devil a foothold." If we harbor anger in our hearts, we open the door for the enemy, giving him a *foothold.* A foothold can best be described as, *a place in your heart you're allowing the enemy to occupy that is reserved for God.*

Think of a time that you were angry with a friend, a sibling, or a parent. The more you focused on the situation, the bigger it became in your mind, because, **whatever you feed, grows.** The more focus you give to your anger, the more that anger begins to wrap around your heart. The devil thrives on the anger in your life. When you hold anger in your heart it produces the perfect breeding ground for the lies of the enemy to be planted. Once the enemy has gained a foothold in your life, a stronghold develops in your heart. Remember *a stronghold* is, *any negative thought pattern that disagrees with God's Word*. Once you begin to *think thoughts* that disagree with God's Word, it's just a matter of time before you *take action* that's in direct opposition to God's Word.

If you're wondering what anger can do if left unattended, just turn on the news. Every day there's a news story about a teen stabbing their parents to death; a mom or dad beating their infant child to death, or someone walking into a school or church and randomly shooting people. Unresolved anger is one of the driving forces behind the violence we witness daily.

Human anger does not produce the righteousness that God desires, James 1:20.

There is a direct connection between your actions and what's in your heart. We've all experienced hurt in our lives. We've had those we love break our hearts—leaving us feeling betrayed, rejected and for some, abandoned. At the moment an offense takes place—we have a choice to make—will we hold out our hands and release the hurt to God, or will we close our fist tightly and hold on to the hurt we've just experienced? As I watch the nightly news, I see how a regular person—just like you and me—was working a stable job one day, and the next he murdered the boss who fired him. What happens in the heart and mind of a person that leads to such an unimaginable act? The answer is locked away in a heart that has been tangled up for years with unresolved anger—anger that began with one lie of the enemy. You cannot afford to hold on to your anger. You were not created to carry the heaviness that anger brings. Anger distorts the words of others; it magnifies the offense of another, and it disconnects you from the life of peace that God desires you to have. Anger shatters your communication with others and tears apart relationships in your life. Anger will steal your joy, kill your dreams, and destroy your relationships. The Bible says, "The thief comes only to steal and kill and destroy; I have come that they may have life, and have it to the full," **John 10:10**.

Take responsibility for the anger you experience.

When I was younger, I often used the phrase, "They make me so mad." As I grew into adulthood, I continued using this phrase—until I experienced one little deception from the enemy. Let me explain. I began to believe that others could make me mad, and it was their actions or words that caused the emotions or feelings that occupied my heart. Now, the *fact* is, yes, others do have the capability to affect your attitude, mood, and emotions, but the **truth** is, *you don't have to give them permission to do so*. When you hold bitterness and resentment in your heart, it soon turns to anger. You either allow anger to have power over your emotions—which is the same as giving the person who hurt you *power*—or you can choose to give the anger to God, and ask Him what the truth is about the situation.

As I sat praying one morning—with conflict in my mind

and turmoil in my heart—I began to ask the Lord why I had no joy. I couldn't understand why I was in constant turmoil and filled with discontent. As the tears rolled down my face, and I searched desperately for an answer to this chaos in my heart, the Lord gently whispered this request to me, "Give me the anger of your past, and I'll give you the hope for your future."

Today, God is whispering the same request to you. God is holding out His hands, waiting for you to bring Him all the offenses that produced the anger you hold onto so tightly. Will you give God the anger of your past—will you let Him give you hope for your future? Hope that assures you that God will make all things right; He will take the hurt of your past and give you a new present. That present is a promise of God's faithfulness.

Anger is an emotion you will walk through when faced with times of injustice. You may be one of those who has been violated in ways unfathomable. Anger is a normal response to the injustice that has occurred. If this is you, and you find yourself filled with overwhelming anger, you are not alone. God understands when it takes time to process the injustice done to you. You must begin to heal from the offense committed. He gives you the grace to walk the road to freedom—as you daily lean on Him.

LISTENING TO THE VOICE OF GOD:

1. God wants to set you free from the past. Will you lean into His touch and lay hold of His truth?

2. Ask God if there is an event in your life, brought about anger, that you have been holding in your heart.

3. Ask God if there is a lie you've believed that has given the devil a foothold in your life. Ask yourself, *What's the truth about this anger I am holding onto?*

4. Ask God what He wants you to do the next time you experience the emotion of *anger* in your life.

TODAY'S DECLARATION:

I will choose today to give the anger of my past to the God of my present.

DAY 13

GOD'S PERFECT PLAN—SALVATION

Everyone who calls on the name of the Lord will be saved, **Romans 10:13.**

What is salvation? What does it mean when you hear someone say they *are saved*? I like to refer to salvation as, *God's perfect plan.* Long before you and I were ever created, God knew the events that would take place—and that those events would bring about devastating consequences. Those events would require a plan to bring God's children back to Him. So, He set out to put the greatest plan there ever would be, in motion. This perfect plan—SALVATION—is available to *whosoever will!*

There are two questions I want to unpack: *Why do we need to be saved; and what are we being saved from?* To answer these two questions we will need to take a trip back to the very beginning. It all started when God created the world. You may be familiar with the story of the creation, and if you are, a song might have just popped into your head! One that goes something like this—*Day one, God made the sun when there was none.* I'll spare you the rest of the song! Let's skip over to the sixth day—the day God created man in His own image—which is found in **Genesis, Chapter One.**

It's important to understand that when God created the Earth and created man in His image, there was no sin. You've heard the saying, "all good things must come to an end." I'm not sure that statement is completely reliable, but in this case, it's true. Do you remember the next series of events? God created Adam and placed him in the Garden of Eden. Adam would work in the garden and take care of it. As the story goes, the Lord decided that it was not good for Adam to be alone, so He caused Adam to fall into a deep sleep. While Adam was sleeping, God took a rib from his side, and from the rib, He created the woman called, Eve.

Ah, the perfect romance! Not so fast! As with any relationship, there were complications that arose. Adam and Eve were hanging out in The Garden when along came the crafty serpent. God had given Adam and Eve specific instructions about the trees in the garden. There was only one tree that was off limits—*the tree of the knowledge of good and evil.* "But you must not eat from the tree of the knowledge of good and evil, for when you eat of it you will surely die," **Genesis 2:17.** As the story continues, the crafty serpent, also known as Satan, poses the one question that would seal the fate of every human—*did God really say?* (**Genesis 3:1**). In a moment of weakness, Eve allowed temptation to override the consequences—*and she took a bite!* Not only did she take a bite, she shared the forbidden fruit with Adam. It was in that moment that sin entered the world—mankind would forever be separated from God and doomed to Hell. However, God, in His great love for us made a plan that provided a way of back to Him.

You might be wondering what a snake, fruit, and a human have to do with salvation?

It was the chain reaction of **temptation**, **deception** and a **choice** that would open the door for sin to enter into the world. "Therefore, just as sin entered the world through one man, and death through sin, and in this way death came to all people, because all sinned," **Romans 5:12**.

It was the disobedience of Adam and Eve that brought sin into the world and separated them from a relationship with God. Adam and Eve's decision did not catch God off-guard—He already knew what choice would be made that day in the Garden. Therefore, God had the *perfect plan* ready to put into motion—one that would allow us the opportunity to once again be in relationship with Him. This plan would come at a high price—it would cost God His one and only Son. "For God so loved the world, that he gave his one and only son, that whoever believes in him shall not perish but have eternal life," **John 3:16**.

Just take a moment to let that sink in. God loved you so much that He was willing to sacrifice His only Son and send Him to die in your place. "God made him who had no sin to be sin for us, so that in him we might become the righteousness of God," **2 Corinthians 5:21**. God looked away as His only son was ridiculed, mocked, spit on, beaten, tortured, nailed to a cross and left to die. A loving Father, with a love so great for you and me, sent His only Son to become sin and take our place on the cross. "But God demonstrates his own love for us in this: While we were still sinners,

Christ died for us," **Romans 5:8**.

The beauty of salvation is that it doesn't require you to do anything. All that is required is total surrender—and it's your **choice**. Will you say, "Yes," to God and His will for your life and will you say, "No," to the world's ways? You don't have to clean up your *messy* life, work hard enough, or be good in order to earn your salvation. Salvation is a gift to those who will accept it. Salvation is *received*, not *achieved*. "For it is by grace you have been saved, through faith—and this is not from yourselves, it is the gift of God," **Ephesians 2:8**.

If you declare with your mouth, "Jesus is Lord," and believe in your heart that God raised him from the dead, you will be saved, **Romans 10:9**.

Let's talk about what it means to be separated from God. God has given each of us a free will. We get to decide who or what we will follow. Before I started studying God's Word, I had this faulty way of thinking about Heaven and Hell. I believed that if you were good enough, you would make it to Heaven—and if you didn't make the cut, you were sent to Hell. I want to share with you the life-altering truth that I have since learned. God's heart is that all His children would choose to turn towards Him and desire to spend eternity with Him. "The Lord is not slow in keeping his promise, as some understand slowness. Instead, he is patient with you, not wanting anyone to perish, but everyone to come to repentance," **2 Peter 3:9**. Unfortunately, there are many who will choose to go their own way instead of surrendering to God's will. The compassionate God we serve doesn't send a person to hell; a person chooses where he or she will go. "But each one is tempted when, by his own evil desire, he is dragged away and enticed," **James 1:14**.

Salvation promises us eternal life with God. God has prepared a place for every believer—a place where there will be no more tears, no more fears, and no more pain. "He will wipe away every tear from their eyes. There will be no more death or mourning or crying or pain, for the old order of things has passed away. I am making everything new!" **Revelation 21:4-5**. That sounds like a place where I want to go!

Salvation also promises us the gift of the Holy Spirit.

Notice I said the "gift" of the Holy Spirit. Just as your salvation is a free gift from God, so it is with the gift of the Holy Spirit. You can't earn these gifts—they are free of charge. The price has already been paid for you and me. The Holy Spirit's job is to guide you into all the truth, He is your counselor, and He is your comforter, (**John 14:26** AMP). Another benefit of this free gift of salvation is 24-hour access the God of the universe. There is never a busy signal—you can access the Holy Spirit whenever you call!

Just as one choice of disobedience separated Adam and Eve from their intimate relationship with God—one choice will either separate us or restore us back into relationship with God. **This choice is called Salvation.** The Bible says, "Everyone who calls on the name of the Lord will be saved," **Romans 10:13**. What does calling on the Lord look like? For me, calling on the Lord came while I was in a state of brokenness. I had finally come to the end of myself and acknowledged my need for a Savior. I could no longer do things the way I had always done them. I was self-destructing at a rapid pace. I wanted to change and it became very apparent that I couldn't do it on my own. I was ready to do business with God.

If you, too, find yourself in a desperate place, not knowing how you are going to continue walking the road you're on, make a decision today to surrender to God. Give up trying to control your life and start relying on God's wisdom to guide your steps. It doesn't matter what you've done, God is standing with His arms wide open, waiting to accept you into His family.

If you have never accepted Jesus Christ into your heart, you can do that this very minute, right where you are.

There are three steps to salvation:

- First, **admit** that you have sinned, repent—which means to exchange your ways for God's ways—and tell God that you're tired of doing things your way. Ask God to forgive you of your sins.

- Second, **believe** that Jesus died on the cross for your sins; and that all your sins were crucified with Jesus.

- Finally, **claim** Jesus as your Lord and Savior. You do this by surrendering your will and choosing His way for your life.

The Bible says, "If you confess with your mouth that Jesus is Lord and believe in your heart that God raised him from the dead, you will be saved," **Romans 10:9**.

If you're ready to make that decision today and are not sure how to pray, I have prepared this simple prayer to help get you started on your new journey with Christ.

Dear Lord, I admit that I have disobeyed and sinned against You. I repent and ask You to forgive me of all my sins. I believe that Jesus died on the cross for my sins and rose again. I surrender my will to You, Jesus, and ask You to come into my heart and be the Lord and Savior of my life. Thank You for saving me and giving me abundant life on earth and eternal life with You. I ask all these things in Jesus Name. AMEN

The choice to follow God is the most important decision you will ever make. Now that you have asked Jesus to be your Lord and Savior the Bible says you are a new creation. "Therefore, if anyone is in Christ, the new creation has come: The old has gone, the new is here!" **2 Corinthians 5:17**. You now have a new identity. You are no longer defined by your past, present or future sins. As a child of the King, you are robed in righteousness. "For he has clothed me with garments of salvation and arrayed me in a robe of his righteousness," **Isaiah 61:10**.

Now that you are saved, what do you do?

As a Christian, you are called to be light in a dark world. This doesn't mean you have to walk around with a Bible in your hand, quoting scripture. I have to confess, there was a time in my life that I thought my job as a Christian was to go around telling others all about their sins. I don't recommend this approach; you won't win many people to Christ, *and* you will be the most avoided person in the room!

What God began to show me was that He loves when we share His Word with others—but what matters to Him is that we love others. Now, I'm not saying that you aren't to share the Bible. But, let's be honest, it can be awkward to walk up to someone you don't know—or maybe you do—and just start talking about God. So, what do you do? Awkward or not, you are still called to share the truth with others. You use your testimony. Once I realized that sharing my testimony didn't have to be equipped with a power point presentation, it became easy. Sharing my testimony was simply telling *my story* of God's love. Your testimony is your own personal story of how God showed up in your life—and how He changed it.

There is no greater way to tell a person about God's love than to share how faithful He has been in your own life. That's loving others! I'd like to give you an example of how quick and painless sharing a testimony can be. In **The Book of John, Chapter Nine**, there was a man who had been blind since birth. Jesus spits on the ground, made mud with his saliva, and then put the mud on the man's eyes. Jesus then told the man to go, "wash in the Pool of Siloam," (**verse 7**). The man did exactly as Jesus instructed him.

He went and washed his eyes in the pool—and the Bible says, "he came home seeing," (**verse** 7). Others began to notice that this was the same blind man who had been begging on the streets just the day before. They began asking the man how he was able to see—and they also found the man's parents to ask how he had been healed. What I want to point out in this story is that, as big as the miracle was, this man's testimony was summed up in these few words, "I was blind, but now I see." He could have kept his story to himself, but you see when God shows up in your life and does the unexplainable, you can't help but tell everyone around you! Your testimony doesn't have to be wordy, it simply has to tell of the mighty hand of God in your life.

LISTENING TO THE VOICE OF GOD:

1. Practice your testimony. You might start by writing down how your life has changed since you have been saved.

2. Recall a time in your life that God showed up and did something that you didn't expect *and* couldn't explain.

We are to be prepared to share God's Word with others around us each day. I want to encourage you to stand firm in your faith. Let what God has done in your life be a reminder of the power of God. Don't let the enemy silence you—stand up and be proud of your heritage, you belong to God!

Preach the word; be prepared in season and out of season; correct, rebuke and encourage—with great patience and careful instruction, 2 Timothy 4:2.

TODAY'S DECLARATION:

I will share my testimony with those around me, telling them of all the great things God has done in my life.

DAY 14

DEPRESSION, OPPRESSION—
WHAT'S THE CONNECTION?

Depression can be overwhelming and often keeps a Christian from living the life that Christ died to give.

I remember it like it was yesterday. The sky was dark, the rain was steadily coming down and I had just received news that I thought could not be true. I felt like my heart had just shattered into a million pieces, my legs were so weak I could barely stand. I stood staring up at the sky as the rain continued to blend in with the tears streaming down my face. As I cried out to God, the sound of my voice turned into an agonizing yell, "Why?" "What did I do wrong to make this happen?" The lyrics from a song by Casting Crowns which says, "I'll praise you in the Storm," rolled through my mind as the rain continued to pound the pavement. I knew it was the Lord trying to speak to my broken heart. I just couldn't understand how I would ever praise the Lord for the damage my heart had just endured.

As the days turned into weeks, weeks into months and months into years, the depression in my life felt heavier than I could ever imagine. I tried ignoring the symptoms. I pushed through each day, just waiting for the sun to go down and the day to end. Any joy in my life had disappeared, and the hope I once knew came to a sudden halt. I had lost the will to live. The pain was so real, and the overwhelming depression that accompanied it hovered over me like a dark cloud.

I tried everything to make the depression go away. I continued living through each day, trying desperately to push away the thoughts that constantly tormented me. I stuck with the one thing I loved to do more than anything else—and that was my running. I remember the day the Lord met me on my run—and how He revealed a truth that began the healing process in my life. As I ran, trying to choke back tears so that I could breathe, the Lord so gently spoke to my heart. I so clearly heard these words, "It's okay to be mad at Me." My run came to a jolting halt as I replayed the words I had just heard, "It's okay to be mad at Me." Did I hear that right? Was God giving me permission to be mad at Him? Yes, that's exactly what God was doing that day. Not only was He giving me permission to be mad at Him—He was giving me *the truth* I needed to send the enemy of my soul packing.

I had been holding on to so much pain that I had nowhere else to place my anger. I was mad at everyone involved in the situation—but there was Someone else at the top of the list. The One

I didn't think I was allowed to be mad at, was the very One I was most angry with. I finally felt I could ask God, *Why didn't You stop what happened? Why did it have to be me that had to deal with such heartbreak?*

Until that day, I didn't understand what oppression was, or how it was playing a part in my life—how it was wreaking havoc with my heart. Oppression comes from the enemy and hinders a believer's ability to serve God with a strong testimony. The enemy was using depression to oppress/weigh me down. and it was working! I had lost my zest for life. I no longer wanted to go to church; I had to make myself pray, and I was losing ground at a rapid pace. *There was a direct connection between the depression I was experiencing and the oppression the enemy was using to hold me down—and it was rendering me ineffective for the Kingdom of God.* "The Lord is a stronghold for the oppressed, a stronghold in times of trouble," **Psalm 9:9.**

I don't know what you're going through, but I do know the pain of depression. I know how it hinders us, as believers, from walking confidently in the truth of who we are in Christ. Depression produces a sense of hopelessness in your life and it keeps you from experiencing the abundant life Christ died to give you. If that's you, don't allow the enemy to steal one more day! Cry out to God—asking Him to come into your circumstances—all the while exposing the enemy's lies. Depression is real and can be debilitating. There are times when we need to see a doctor to diagnose the symptoms we experience. Don't be ashamed if you need to reach out for help—simply ask God to show you what He would have you do.

God will reveal to you absolute truth—truth that will expel the darkness in your life.

King David knew all too well what depression does to the soul. David cried out to the Lord in a time of depression, "Why, my soul, are you downcast? Why so disturbed within me? Put your hope in God for I will yet praise him, my Savior and my God," **Psalm 42:11**. David is wrestling with the heaviness in his life—but, as quickly as he questions the heaviness, he recalls the answer. David knew that the only way to silence the enemy was to place his absolute hope and trust in God. The same is true for you and me. When we begin to feel the darkness moving in, we must immediately turn our focus onto the goodness of God. Remember that your hope is not in your circumstances, your hope is in the Lord and the power of His rising!

LISTENING TO THE VOICE OF GOD:

1. Ask God to show you an event in your life that has allowed the enemy an open door into your life. What does God want you to know about the specific event He has shown you?

2. Depression is real and can take us into dark places in our lives. Ask the Lord if there is something in your heart that is causing the enemy to hold you down. Ask the Lord what He wants to give you in exchange.

TODAY'S DECLARATION:

I will shout of God's goodness and all that He's done!

DAY 15

SECURITY CHECKPOINT— WHAT WILL YOU ALLOW TO COME AND GO?

If your words were the final words a person would ever hear—what would they have heard you say?

It seemed harmless—just a phone and a little *Snapchat* story. After all, no one got hurt—or did they? As I sat on the floor, across from my teenage son, watching the tears roll down his face, I choked back my own tears. I was praying I could maintain my composure and speak the words of encouragement needed to soothe his breaking heart. As he wiped away the tears, he began to share with me the false accusations his "friends" had posted across social media—and the rumors that he couldn't outrun.

As I sat, silently listening for God to drop the perfect words into my heart, my son disappeared for a split-second. He quickly returned, only to place a sharp object into my hand. My heart broke into a million pieces as I listened to the next words out of his mouth, "Mom, you can have this (knife); I laid awake last night thinking about using it." His words shook me to my very core. As I began to process those words, in the midst of my mother's rage, I realized the power our words hold—not only in our own lives, but also in the lives others.

I am forever grateful my son had the courage to share with us the deep hurt that he'd been carrying.

I am thankful God protected my son from the enemy's lies—lies that tormented him with the thought that his life was no longer worth living. Kids of all ages are taking their own lives at an alarming rate—often due to the reckless words spoken from a peer. It's no joke, *words wound!* Words have the power to hurt, and *yes*, more times than we'd like to admit, *words have the power to kill!* The words we speak contain power. Our words have the power to build up or tear down. It's time to start searching our hearts before we speak. The Bible speaks of the tongue as *a restless evil, full of poison*. That's a pretty strong description for something so small. "Likewise, the tongue is a small part of the body, but it makes great boasts. Consider what a great forest is set on fire by a small spark," **James 3:5.**

Our words are motivated by our thoughts. Just listen to a person's words, and you'll discover the condition of their heart.

In **Psalm 139:23**, David requests that God search his heart. Why would this be something David would ask of God? Did David know the secret to staying closely connected to God? David was referred to as, "a man after God's own heart," (**Acts 13:22**). I have found in my own life, walking intimately with God requires a clean and accessible heart. David understood that his heart was a storage container and whatever he allowed in or out directly influenced his connection with God.

Have you heard the story of David and Bathsheba? Their story began *in the spring of the year, the time when kings go out to battle*, (**2 Samuel 11:1**). David, after deciding not to go out to battle with his men, found himself in the wrong place, thinking the wrong thoughts. As the story goes, David was out walking on his roof one evening when he looked into the distance and saw a beautiful woman bathing—her name was Bathsheba. In that moment, David had a choice to make. He needed to stop and examine his thoughts. He had the choice to be honorable and not entertain the lustful thoughts or he could allow his mind to take him down the wrong path. David allowed his fleshly desire to override his spiritual discernment. His thoughts had a direct impact on the next action he would take. Our thoughts take us where we're going.

I spent years wrestling with my thoughts. Self-doubt and self-loathing became the premier thought patterns in my day. Every thought was filled with such negativity that it became my normal. If I did have a positive thought, it sure didn't take long before a negative one showed up to take its place. Now, for some people, thinking positively might come easy, but for me, it was a full-time job. I never felt that anything was right in my life. I looked for things to be wrong; and if things were right, I'd began to think of all the ways they could go wrong. Never knowing that I could take control over the thoughts I allowed to enter my mind, I spent day after day in a battle with myself. The sad reality is, I wasted way too much time and energy staying in that vicious cycle of defeat.

God revealed to me that my thoughts were directly affecting my attitude; my attitude was producing my words, and my words were influencing my actions. I began to claim certain thoughts as my own: "Out of the overflow of the heart the mouth speaks," **Luke 6:45**. This scripture became a huge truth in my life. I had allowed the lies of the enemy to have direct influence over *my thoughts* and *my words*. I had unknowingly *come* into agreement with the lies of the enemy.

Recently, God asked me this question, "Are your thoughts producing *joy* or *junk?*" As I pondered my answer, I began to think of my computer mailbox. Each day I receive new emails—some appear in my inbox and many more appear in my *junk* folder. I wonder why they didn't just name it, *some things you might want to read*, instead of *junk?* Anyway, God began to show me how my thoughts are similar to the mail that appears in my mailbox. If I choose to read anything that is in my junk mail folder, I first have to mark it safe. Once I mark it safe, it is moved to my inbox. If I take the time to check my mailbox each day, why don't I take the same precautionary measures with my mind—scanning my thoughts before accepting them as *safe?*

Your mind is like that email mailbox, holding a ton of information daily. Some information is safe and needed, while much more information is worthless, and needs to be deleted.

Do you stop and think about what you're thinking about?

What if every day you took the time to ask yourself this one question: *Is this what God would say?* If the answer is, *No*, then throw out the junk! The Bible says that we, "demolish arguments and every pretension that sets itself up against the knowledge of God, and we take captive every thought to make it obedient to Christ," **2 Corinthians 10:5**. You are to demolish and take captive any thought that does not agree with the Word of God. In order to demolish an argument, you must have viable truth with which to fight. What does it mean to take something captive? To take something captive you have to catch it and forcefully hold onto it.

You have the option to accept a thought or reject a thought. The moment a thought drops into your mind ask yourself, *Is this something God would say?* If the answer is, *no*, then you must immediately demolish the argument with the truth. The battle in your mind is won with the truth of God's Word. This is the most powerful weapon you have against the enemy of your soul.

Much like our thoughts, our words also contain power. Words are like weapons; they can build up or tear down. The Bible says, "Life and death are in the power of the tongue," **Proverbs 18:21.** *What we allow into our hearts is reflected in the words we speak, and guides the direction our lives will take.* "Above all else, guard your heart, for everything you do flows from it," **Proverbs 4:23**.

Guard your heart and your mind; you are the gatekeeper. Choose your words carefully. When the enemy speaks a lie to you, counter with the truth. Confess the truth daily, even if it's completely opposite of the way you feel. Come into agreement with the truth of God's Word each day. Speak the Word out loud; let the enemy know whose side you're on! "A good man brings good things out of the good stored up in his heart, and an evil man brings evil things out of the evil stored up in his heart. For the mouth speaks what the heart is full of," **Luke 6:45**.

LISTENING TO THE VOICE OF GOD:

1. What are some thoughts that you struggle with daily?

2. Ask God to reveal to you any lies you have been agreeing with. Ask God to show you the truth—write down the truth you are shown.

3. What can you do each day to align your thoughts and words with God's truth?

TODAY'S DECLARATION:

I will align my thoughts, words, and actions to the truth of God's Word.

DAY 16

RESTING IN HIM—
FREEDOM FROM RELIGION

When I was fifteen I decided I would go on *a mission trip*. It was a Wednesday night and we were meeting to go over a few things for the trip. The moment I walked into the room, I had this overwhelming feeling that I didn't belong. It didn't take me long to figure out why. As I sat there, I began to look around the room—and I wondered if I was as spiritual or religious as the others. And then it happened! The instructor said, "Get out your Bibles." You're probably thinking to yourself, "What's wrong with that?" The Bible I had in front of me hadn't been opened very much. The feeling of inadequacy flooded my soul. We were told we needed to memorize scriptures—not just one, but multiple scriptures! I didn't think I could find the various books of the Bible, never mind memorize that many scriptures. Thank goodness for the concordance at the back of the Bible! For me, concordance was just a fancy name for, *"All those who are clueless look here."*

I left that night feeling utterly defeated. I truly wanted to go on a mission trip. I had a strong desire to help others—but after that night, I simply wanted to go home and crawl in a hole. I allowed the thought, *in order to please God, I need to memorize a bunch of scriptures,* to be planted in my heart. In order for God to love me and be pleased, I believed I would need to work really hard to "be good enough." The problem with this thinking—as I learned much later—is that it is impossible to "be good enough" in my own strength.

I spent the rest of my years throughout high school and college, not only trying to be good enough but most often trying to be *perfect*. I hope you know there is no such thing as perfect! Striving for perfection is the most draining job in the world. Once you think you've reached the top, you find there is still another mountain you have to climb.

What if I told you that God isn't looking for perfect?

God isn't even looking for you to "do" all the right things. I hope, by now, you're scratching your head and wondering, "Then what *does* God want from me?" God wants you to rest. Yes, I said rest! There are several verses in the Bible that talk about resting. The rest the Lord speaks of in His Word comes from having an intimate, personal relationship with Him. A relationship that is built on truth. When we are trusting in God, we can rest—knowing that He is at work in our lives.

I have to confess that I struggle a lot in this area. I want to know *why, how and when* for every event that happens in my life. As I spend countless hours trying to, "figure things out," I am forfeiting my *rest* for confusion and frustration. The Lord gave me an acronym as a reminder to **R E S T** in Him—trusting that every step is strategically timed.

Reassured Every Step is Timed

In **Matthew 23**, Jesus was addressing the Pharisees— a pious group of religious men who thought they kept all God's rules. The Pharisees did not like what Jesus taught. They thought they were better than everyone else, because in their own minds they never did anything wrong. "But do not do what they do, for they do not practice what they preach. They tie up heavy loads and put them on men's shoulders, but they themselves are not willing to lift a finger to move them. Woe to you, teachers of the law and Pharisees, you hypocrites! You are like whitewashed tombs, which look beautiful on the outside, but on the inside are full of dead men's bones and everything unclean. In the same way you, on the outside you appear to people as righteous but on the inside, you are full of hypocrisy and wickedness," **Matthew 23:27-28**.

Jesus came to explain that following rules and regulations only produces religious attitudes. What Jesus was trying to get them to understand was that we are to *love Him and love others*. Does this mean that God doesn't care if we do the wrong thing? He most certainly cares, but He does not quit loving us when we mess up. *Religion is based on "doing"—Relationship with the Father is based on "resting" in Him.*

Religion that God our Father accepts as pure and faultless is this: to look after orphans and widows in their distress (those that need help) and to keep oneself from being polluted by the world, James 1:27.

Are you receiving or achieving? Are you resting or working to obtain God's love?

One way to answer these questions is to ask more questions. Ask yourself, *Am I worn out and exhausted from trying to be perfect and do everything right?* Ask yourself how you view God, *Do I see God as a loving Father, One Who wants to speak to me —or do I see a Father who's keeping a record of my mistakes?* You'll notice that one response causes you to *run away* from God, and the other causes you to draw closer to God. One results in a peace that surpasses all understanding while the other brings strife, turmoil, and discontentment.

God loves His children with an *agape* love—an unconditional, unearned and undeserved love—one that we don't work to achieve, we simply rest and receive. Our relationship with God is not based on us trying harder and doing all the right things—it's about surrendering our will in exchange for His way. It's just that simple!

If you are worn out from trying to earn God's love, and you're ready to rest in the unconditional love of The Father, open up your heart and receive His love now.

LISTENING TO THE VOICE OF GOD:

1. Ask God if there's a lie you've believed about God's love for you.

2. Ask God what He wants you to do the next time you start to believe that you have to work to earn His love.

3. Ask God to show you what receiving His love looks like.

TODAY'S DECLARATION:

Today I will receive God's love, not because I have earned it, but because He has freely given it to me.

DAY 17

FAITH—MY FAITH OR YOURS?

I started this run the same as any other—after lacing my shoes, I grabbed my watch and secured my headphones. As I have mentioned, one of my favorite places to run is in the country, where the roads take me *to a place of solitude*. As I set out on the winding roads, I took a quick glance down at my feet—and started thinking about how it was probably time for a new pair of running shoes. The shoes I was wearing had quite a few miles on them, and the tread was wearing thin.

If you are a runner, then you know the importance of having a well-made pair of shoes to support your body while you pound the pavement. As I continued on my run, I scrolled through shoe websites in my mind, shopping for the perfect pair of shoes to buy. As I was pondering the perfect pair of shoes, another question came to mind, *what's one thing that wouldn't be good to purchase used?* I quickly thought, *a pair of running shoes.*

Have you ever been to a resale shop? I love to go to resale

shops. I like to check out all the items that others don't want or just got tired of—and I always find something cool to buy! However, the one thing I would never want to purchase is a used pair of running shoes. Why? Because they have already been *broken down*. Just for fun, try borrowing someone else's shoes for a day. Go about your day as planned, wearing the borrowed shoes. As you do, you will begin to notice that they don't quite fit right. Sure, you could manage to wear them for a while, but soon it will be apparent they aren't yours and frustration will take hold. Maybe you will notice they are rubbing in all the wrong places, or they aren't molding to your foot for a comfortable wear. As the day drags on, what you were able to tolerate, will eventually become an irritation that can no longer be ignored.

As a Christian, our faith can be likened to a pair of running shoes. Every runner knows you need a stable pair of shoes to endure the race. As believers, we need *our own faith*—that comes from *our own experiences* with God—to be able to endure the race that is set before us. Just as a customized pair of running shoes are made to fit your foot perfectly, faith has to be customized by your own encounter with God.

I remember growing up in church—and not understanding most of what I was taught. It's not that what was spoken didn't contain truth, it was that my heart hadn't been prepared to receive the truth. Rather than receive truth for myself, I relied on what my parents told me, and how they lived, as "my faith." The problem is by trying to borrow the faith of another, you will never be stable enough yourself to stand strong in your own faith. God wants your faith solidified, so that when—not if—but, *when* the enemy attacks, you are armed and ready for the battle.

How do you develop a faith of your own? Faith starts by seeking God above all else. "Seek first his kingdom and his righteousness, and all these things will be given to you as well," **Matthew 6:33**. As you surrender your heart to God and begin to seek Him for direction in your life, everything else will begin to fall into place. Seeking God allows you to get to know God. If you want to trust that what God says is true, you must first know Him. How do you get to know God? Spend time with Him. The more time you spend with someone, the more you get to know that person. The same is true of God. "So faith comes from hearing, that is, hearing the Good News about Christ," **Romans 10:17**. The more time you spend listening to others who already know God, reading the truth of God's Word and studying the characteristics of God, the more you begin to know Him.

What would it look like if you started every day with God? There's no limit on the amount of time you can spend with God. You can begin your journey with God by asking Him to reveal Himself to you. God says in His Word, "If you look for me wholeheartedly, you will find me," **Jeremiah 29:13**.

You need your own faith so that you can be a light in a dark world. You need to know the truth on which your faith is built in order to represent the goodness of God daily. *Fan the flame of faith in your life and make it grow!*

LISTENING TO THE VOICE OF GOD:

1. Describe what *faith* means to you? Do you have your own faith?

2. As you seek God, ask Him what He wants you to know about Him.

3. Ask God what you can do each day to grow closer to Him.

We will overcome, by the blood of the lamb and the word of our testimony. **Revelation 12:11**

TODAY'S DECLARATION:

I will spend time each day allowing God to build and stretch my faith in Him. When the lies of the enemy come against me, I will use my own faith to expose those lies and reveal the truth of God's Word.

DAY 18

PRAYER—24 HOURS A DAY, 7 DAYS A WEEK

With my eyes closed and my head bowed, I waited for the longest prayer I'd ever heard to come to an end. *What was he saying, and why was he taking so long to say it? Couldn't he make his point?* My neck was stiff and my eyes were crossing from the strain of trying to look around, without lifting my head. Surely others were relating to what I was experiencing? I often dreaded the words, "would you bow your head in prayer." Each Sunday morning the same old guy in the gray suit would make his way to the pulpit, and commence to pray a marathon prayer. During my teenage years, those words were an invitation not to speak with God, but to take a needed nap.

Pardon my honesty, but back then I wasn't taught the power of prayer—it was simply "the thing" we did at a certain time and in a certain way. I spent a lot of years pondering that thought. I heard *about* prayer growing up, but never taught *how* to pray or *why* I should pray. It's hard to do something you don't know how to do. It's especially hard to do something when you're not quite sure why you should do it. I knew I should pray, but I wasn't really sure where to begin.

Have you ever struggled to understand prayer?

Have you pondered the *what, who and why* behind prayer? If this is you, help is on the way. I want to teach you a few things that revolutionized the way I viewed prayer.

The first thing you need to know is this—***prayer is a conversation with God***. Think about how you engage in conversation with those around you. Listening is a vital component of being fully engaged in conversation. Listening requires your undivided attention. To hear what another is saying, you must remove yourself from every distraction and become fully aware of the person you are in conversation with. The same is true when you speak with God in prayer. You must stay aware of His presence and engage Him without distractions. One of the most important ways you receive God's truth is through prayer. Prayer is releasing your cares to the Father. The Bible says in **1 Peter 5:7**, "Cast your cares on the Lord, for he cares for you." You were *never* designed to carry the burdens in your life; you were designed to lay them down at the foot of the cross. *Prayer provides the way to transfer the heaviness of your heart into the faithfulness of God's hands.*

Jesus taught His disciples the true meaning of prayer. Using the Lord's Prayer for guidance, He explained how to pray.

Our Father in heaven, hallowed be your name, your king-dom come, your will be done, on earth as it is in heaven. Give us today our daily bread. And forgive us our debts, as we also have forgiven our debtors. And lead us not into temptation, but deliver us from the evil one, **Matthew 6:9-13**.

For you and I, the Lord's Prayer gives us the "ingredients" we need for prayer. As with baking a cake, there are certain ingre-dients that must be added to have the final result—*a delicious cake.* The same can be said of prayer—as you pray you can follow the "ingredients" of the Lord's prayer, using your own words to ex-press your heart to God. Jesus never intended you to use the Lord's prayer as "the prayer" you use each time you pray. If you pray the same way, using the same words each time, you have not connected with God's heart. A memorized series of words have no meaning—leading us to view prayer as a chore, rather than a privilege.

Prayer is something we **get** *to do, not something we* **have** *to do.*

God wants an honest and open heart, not a series of rehearsed words. **God is more concerned with the condition of your heart than the words you choose.** "And when you pray, do not keep on babbling like pagans, for they think they will be heard because of their many words," **Matthew 6:7**. The more you pray, the closer your connection—and the deeper your relationship with God will become.

Prayer is having a conversation with God—it's that simple. When having a conversation with a friend, after speaking, what do you do? You listen for their response. The same is true of your conversation with God. You speak, and then you listen—waiting for God to speak. One of the ways you hear God is through prayer. You must believe by faith that you can hear the voice of God. The Bible says, *my sheep listen to my voice; I know them and they follow me,* **John 10:3-4.** God refers to us as His sheep. Sheep need a shepherd to guide and direct them. God, our shepherd, keeps us close and protects us along the journey of our lives. Sheep learn to recognize their shepherd's voice, and once they do, they follow him. The more we pray, the more we learn to discern our Shepherd's voice.

Prayer is spending time with God. Prayer is opening up your heart, emptying yourself and coming to God in humility. There is no right or wrong way to pray. It's telling God, "Thank You," for how He has blessed you. Prayer is also a time of praising Him for His goodness in your life. The Bible says that we are to lay our requests before Him, (**Psalm 5:3**). Yes, you can ask God for things you *need*—He even likes you to ask Him for the things you *want*. God wants you to have an honest relationship with Him—and that relationship develops through prayer. Having a conversation with God allows you to connect with His heart. He is a personal God; One Who wants to speak with you.

The Bible says, *Devote yourselves to prayer being watchful and thankful,* (**Colossians 4:2**); and *pray continually,* (**1 Thessalonians 5:17**). When I first read these particular verses I thought to myself, *How can anyone pray all the time? It's impossible to pray without ceasing.* As I searched for the meaning of these verses, I began to better understand the thoughts behind these scriptures.

They don't mean I was to actually stop what I was doing and go into my room and pray without *ceasing*. They reflect the condition of your heart and the daily connection you have to God's heart. I learned that I could pray *anywhere* at *anytime*. I can have a conversation in my car; at the store; while I go for a run; as I sit on my porch. Prayer starts with God's presence.

God is omnipresent—He is everywhere—therefore, my prayers are heard anywhere at anytime.

Prayer is powerful! Prayer builds your faith and opens the door for God to work in your life. Prayer strengthens your faith and builds your trust in God. "The prayer of a righteous person is powerful and effective," **James 5:16.** The more I understood the power of prayer, the faster I called on the Lord. I spent years calling my mom the moment things went wrong in my life. I would pour out my heart to her, with tears streaming down my face, begging for the answers to my problems. As I grew in my walk with the Lord, He began to show me that He longed to be first in my life— especially in the area of prayer. He wanted to be the One I ran to in a moment of crisis. He wanted to be the first person I called when a problem arose, or when my heart got broken. He wanted to be the first person I cried out to when the storms of life came, and I couldn't see a way out. He showed me He was—and would be—in the boat always; all I had to do was call on Him in prayer.

I no longer look at prayer as something I have to do to fulfill my Christian calling. I now view prayer as a 24-hour, seven-day-a-week lifeline to the Father. I start and finish all my days talking with God. What I used to view as a chore has now become a privilege in my life.

Here are a few helpful ideas for your prayer life:

REMEMBER...

1. It's not the length of the prayer that matters to God, it's the heart behind the prayer. Open your heart to God. Be honest with God—He already knows.

2. There is no right or wrong time or place to pray as long as God is leading you.

3. Prayer does not require speaking out loud, you can also pray in the stillness of your heart.

4. Prayer begins with a thankful heart. A heart of gratitude prepares you to receive what God wants to say to you as you open your heart to Him with thanksgiving.

5. Prayer is simply a conversation that starts with the words, "Hello God!"

Prayer isn't a series of eloquent words, it's an ongoing conversation with the One Who knows you best.

LISTENING TO THE VOICE OF GOD:

Use the space below to write a letter to God. Start by thanking God for every one of His blessings that come to mind. Next, write what's in your heart. Be honest with God about what's in your heart. As you begin to write, the words will come naturally. Don't think about your wording, simply open your heart and let it flow!

TODAY'S DECLARATION:

I will pour out my heart to God in prayer daily, knowing that He hears me, and can't wait to speak with me.

DAY 19

THE THREE C'S YOU WILL BE GLAD YOU BROUGHT HOME— CONFIDENT, COURAGEOUS & COMMITTED

It's time to stand up for what's right in a world that's gone wrong.

When I was young we used to play the game, "Follow the Leader." One person was at the front of the line, and whatever they did and wherever they went, everyone followed. It was a simple game; one that didn't require much thought. The only requirement was to repeat what you saw the leader doing. Young people today are still playing, "Follow the Leader." Unfortunately, their leaders aren't following the greatest leader of all—Jesus Christ!

We live in a world that makes up the "rules" as we go along. There is no absolute for what is right or wrong, good or bad, acceptable or unacceptable. We blindly follow leaders who are headed in the wrong direction, going down a dead-end road. God is calling all believers to stand up for truth. We must begin taking a stand for what we know is right, regardless of who takes a stand against us.

What makes a good leader—or more importantly, what makes a godly leader?

A godly leader is **confident** no matter the challenge he or she may see before them. In order to stand against opposition, a leader's confidence must be rooted in Christ. Can you think of a time you had the opportunity to stand for Christ? Did you take that opportunity—or should I say, *did you take the risk?*

Taking a stand for Christ can be spelled R-I-S-K. Standing up for the truth is a risky business, but when you stand for Christ you never stand alone. You might risk the ridicule of others or the loneliness that can come with standing up for Christ, but Jesus promises, "he will never leave or forsake us," (**Deuteronomy 31:6**). When we stand firm in our faith as Christ's followers, God will show up and strengthen us for the battle ahead. No matter what is in front of us, we can rest assured God is already there, waiting for us to follow Him with steadfast faith.

The story of Nehemiah is a perfect example of an ordinary man used by God to do extraordinary things. The Bible doesn't say much about Nehemiah's life before he rebuilt the wall of Jerusalem, but what we do learn is that Nehemiah had a heart for God and God's people. He had a servant's heart.

Let me give you a brief overview of the book of Nehemiah. Nehemiah was the Cupbearer to King Artaxerxes. Nehemiah's job was to taste the King's food to prevent the King from being poisoned.

Nehemiah was devastated when he heard the wall of Jerusalem had been broken down and burned. He wept and mourned for Jerusalem. He knew that it was not God's ultimate plan that Jerusalem lay in ruins. He went to King Artaxerxes to receive permission to travel to Jerusalem and rebuild the walls of the devastated city. Rebuilding the wall of Jerusalem would be no small task. Nehemiah could not take on a task this big all by himself. He rallied people from all walks of life and led them in accomplishing something great. The Bible tells us he gathered together goldsmiths, perfume makers, rulers, priests, merchants—everyone who would help.

The wall was divided into sections and everyone took responsibility to fix their part of the torn down wall. There would be opposition and obstacles along the way. Like every good story, there were bad guys. These bad guys plotted against Nehemiah and the people to stop the work of the Lord. The Bible says they mocked Nehemiah and made threats if he didn't stop building. Nehemiah reminded the workers not to be afraid, and to remember the Lord was with them. They didn't allow the opposition of the enemy to cause them to quit. They continued their work with one hand and held a weapon in the other. The rebuilding of the wall was completed in only 52 days.

I believe that God is calling us all to rebuild the walls of our world—the walls of the family, the walls of neighborhoods, and the walls of schools. *What if*, just like Nehemiah, we wept when we saw the injustice of the world? *What if* our hearts broke for the ungodly behavior in our schools? *What if* when we watched our children sit alone during school lunch; or as we saw the rejection inflicted by others, it broke our hearts—the same way it breaks God's heart when His children are mistreated. What if we had a heart like Nehemiah—and no matter what opposition came against us, everywhere we went, we would continue to take a stand for Christ?

You are called to be a representative of Christ—to be His example to those around you. The Bible says you are to be *in* the world, but not *of* it. You are to be light in a dark world. God wants you to take a stand for what is right—even when others are doing wrong. Will this be hard? You bet. Will it be impossible? Absolutely not! The only way you will become a confident leader is to abide or remain rooted in Him. You must follow the example Christ has set for you. A confident leader knows *who* they are and *Whose* they are. Confidence does not come from what you can accomplish on your own, but rather what God can accomplish through you.

Nehemiah wasn't worried about what others thought or said; he remained focused and obedient to what God had called him to do. Just as Nehemiah remained connected to the One Who provided the plan, God's opinion must matter more in your life than the opinion of others. When you truly believe that God's opinion is the only one that matters, you will be able to stand confidently against all opposition.

Here are the Three C's you will be glad you brought home:

CONFIDENT

A confident leader is prayerful, leads by example, has a servant's heart, and is obedient. When God calls you to do something for

Him, you can remain confident that He will give you the tools you need. Nehemiah was asked to rebuild the walls of Jerusalem. Even though he faced opposition and was mocked, he continued to obey God—and the Lord gave him favor. Just like Nehemiah, your confidence, and your Identity must remain rooted in God. Your trust must be in God's ability, not your own ability. You can trust God's goodness in your life and know that when God says, "Stand," He will be standing with you. No matter what came against Nehemiah, he knew who was for him—and you need to know who is for you—GOD! "If God be for us, who can be against us?" **Romans 8:31.**

COURAGEOUS

A courageous person will take authority against the enemy. Courage stands against the fear and the lies of the enemy. Courage says, *"I will,"* when everything in you wants to say, *"I won't."* When the enemy came against Nehemiah and his people, they continued to walk in their calling. Remember, they didn't stop and start panicking because the enemy was pursuing them, they continued on, *working with one hand, with a weapon in the other.* Let's be like Nehemiah and start taking a stand no matter what others say or do. A courageous leader keeps walking even when faced with fear.

COMMITTED

A committed leader is dedicated, loyal and devoted to God and His ways. You are able to be committed to God when you are connected to God's heart. Nehemiah remained committed to following God because he stayed connected to God's heart. He didn't let what he saw change what he knew to be true. He stayed plugged into his ultimate power source, further allowing him to complete the job he had been sent to do.

A godly leader remains confident, courageous and committed by placing their total trust in God. As you place your trust in God, you will begin to see things as He sees them. Your humility will be seen by all. As a leader in Christ, it is not your strength that allows you to stand for Him, but rather it is His strength working in you and through you to accomplish His will.

Am I now trying to win the approval of human beings, or of God? Or am I trying to please people? If I were still trying to please people, I would not be a servant of Christ, **Galatians 1:10.**

LISTENING TO THE VOICE OF GOD:

1. Write out some ways that you can start leading right where you are.

2. What can you do to take a stand for Christ?

TODAY'S DECLARATION:

I will not allow opposition to stop me from being a confident, courageous and committed leader—or from fulfilling God's plan and purpose in my life.

DAY 20

DON'T FORGET WHO YOU ARE

At the heart of every person is the need to be **loved, affirmed, accepted** and **chosen**. Throughout the writing of this book, I have been thrust into places and situations that have given me the needed experiences to complete my writing. I have personally been challenged by the words and the lessons I have written about. Here are a few of the lessons I have learned and would like to pass along to you:

LESSON #1
Identity is not *what I do*, but *who I am* that matters. I felt challenged as I sat staring at a room of teenagers—who were all staring straight back at me. The words, "You're just a substitute," would taunt me as the glaring teen eyes were fixed in my direction, with unrelenting skepticism. I couldn't help but feel a total lack of acceptance from the other teachers, challenging my status—and my ability. The unspoken opinion of others found their way into a vul-

nerable place in my heart—the place of my self-worth. My identity was in question—and a high level of insecurity swept over me. Would I allow the enemy to use my own words against me, or would I believe what God had spent years teaching me? Could I stand against the old lie that always said, *I'm not enough?* I have learned *I can* stand tall in the truth of God's Word that tells me, *I am enough—because HE did enough!*

LESSON #2

Hearing God—*did I or didn't I?* I was speechless when faced with a teenage girl crying over the news of her friend being diagnosed with cancer. I gently laid my hand on her back, showing her I cared and was there for her. I struggled for what seemed like hours—in reality only a couple of minutes—to try to find the words to tell her that everything would be okay. *Where should I begin*, I thought? So I did what any unprepared person would do, I asked her about her friend. I said, "Does your friend know God?" She implied "yes," with a simple nod of her head, as the tears continued to stream down her face. I then asked her if she, too, knew God. The answer I received brought the conversation to a screeching halt. "No, I don't believe in God," she replied.

As I gathered my thoughts, I began scrambling for what to say. I wasn't sure if I should end the conversation on that note, or try to speak about the Jesus I knew? I felt as if I was straining to hear God. I thought, *Do I continue to talk about you, God?* I don't remember a lot about the rest of the conversation. I do know that my heart was grieved as I walked away, believing I had failed at sharing the Gospel with her. As I walked away, I asked the Lord, "How will she ever meet You, if I can't find the words to tell her about You?" Just as quickly as I asked the question, the answer washed over my heart, "She met Me when she met you."

I learned that day that I didn't have to have all my words in order—I just had to have a heart like Christ. The words will come when they are needed. The Bible reassures me of that in **Jeremiah 1:9**, "Then the Lord reached out his hand and touched my mouth and said to me, "I have put my words in your mouth."

The story wasn't over there. The next day I received a phone call from one of the principals at the school where I taught. The mother of the student from the previous day was unhappy that I mentioned God to her daughter. Let's just say it, *she was offended.* I was told that we were not allowed to share our faith with students. As I hung up the phone, a burning flame of anger rolled over me. I spent the next few hours stewing over the conversation. *Why couldn't I just let it go and accept the reprimand?* And then **Lesson #3** was offered—I was embarrassed and ashamed that I had even mentioned God. *Maybe I shouldn't have said a word*, I thought to myself. Before that thought could be completed in my mind, I was interrupted with these words, " I am not ashamed of the gospel."

LESSON #3

I am not *ever* to be ashamed or afraid to share the good news of Christ's love—even when faced with opposition! "For I am not ashamed of the gospel, because it is the power of God that brings salvation to everyone who believes," **Romans 1:16**.

LESSON #4

Faith can be *shaken*, but not *taken*. I've been tempted many times over these last few days to declare defeat. As a matter of fact, I did utter defeat with the words I spoke as I sat on the floor of my closet and cried. Mine were tears of defeat—and my pounding head was proof that the enemy had beat me to a pulp that day. As I wiped away the tears, I reminded myself that *defeat is permanent, but a bad day is temporary*. Even though I had a miserable day, and the enemy swooped in to see if I was ready to raise my white flag as a symbol of surrender, I was not defeated. Each and every day I clothe myself in God's armor—so that *when* the enemy stands ready to attack—I stand ready to defend. I won't allow the enemy to use my bad day as a day of defeat, but rather a day of lessons learned—lessons which bring me closer to my destiny.

LESSON #5

A dream from God will always involve a journey—*with a few un-answered questions*. I recall a certain individual in the Bible who had a dream. You may be familiar with him, as well? Joseph was the youngest of all his brothers. He was just seventeen when the Lord spoke to him in a dream. Joseph just had to tell his brothers about the dream, "Listen to this dream I had. We were all out in the field gathering bundles of wheat. All of a sudden my bundle stood straight up and your bundles circled around it and bowed down to mine." His brothers said, "So! You're going to rule us?" Then Joseph had another dream and told this one to his brothers as well: "I dreamed another dream—the sun and moon and eleven stars bowed down to me!" (**Genesis 37:6-9**)

If you're familiar with the story, then you remember that this dream took many years to become reality. Joseph endured many unfortunate events in his life—all of which would ultimately lead him to his final destination. He was sold into slavery by his brothers, falsely accused by Potiphers' wife, and finally, imprisoned. During all the hardships Joseph faced, his broken heart must have questioned the Lord's goodness. Yet, all these tragic events were used by the Lord to bring Joseph into God's perfect plan—the purpose for which he was created.

What kept Joseph going when everything in his life was falling apart? I'm sure the dream God had given him seemed to move further away with every unfortunate event that occurred. In spite of everything, Joseph held on to a truth that was forever sealed in his heart: *God is good all the time—even when bad things happen. God's timing is perfect—even when expectations appear to be unmet.* As the story comes to a close, God uses all the trials that Joseph endured to bring "the dream" into reality. The realization of that dream would show the glory of God to the Nations. Joseph didn't allow the opposition he faced to destroy the *truth* he held deep in his heart.

Not a moment of your life is wasted.

There isn't a tear that's been shed, that God doesn't hold it in the palm of His hand. What the enemy has used in your life for harm, the Lord promises that *He* will work it all for good! Don't allow another lie of the enemy to keep you from pressing forward into all God has for you. Keep standing on the truth and declaring daily the promises that God has given you.

TODAY'S DECLARATION:

I will not allow the enemy to derail me from the destiny that awaits me!

DAY 21

THE ULTIMATE CHALLENGE!

Now that you've connected with God's heart, it's time to connect with the heart of those closest to you. Today is the day you'll look back over the 21-day journey and recall the truth of what God has spoken to you. Spend time daily allowing God to fill your heart with His truth. Each day make it a point to speak words of life—over yourself and all those you encounter. Let your words be seasoned with encouragement, affirmation and love. You are *uniquely made with a purpose*. Celebrate the person God has created you to be. You have so much to offer. Focus on the unique gifts and talents that God has given you and use them to bring Him glory.

I pray that these last 21 days have been life-changing for you.

As you can see by now, the theme of *Destiny Walking: The 21 Day Freedom Challenge*, is all about connecting your heart to the heart of God. Discovering who God created you to be; claiming the authority you have been given in Christ; and walking in the destiny He has called you to. *When you connect to the heart of God, He begins to unfold and reveal to you the absolute truth about who you are and where He is.* As you continue your freedom journey, remember, "where the spirit of the Lord is, there is freedom," **2 Corinthians 3:17**. I pray that you will start each day more aware of God's presence in your life. Each day ask God to strengthen you for the tasks ahead and to remind you of who you are—His child— His masterpiece. As you continue seeking God with all your heart, He will continue directing the path of your journey.

God has called you to be light in a dark world. I'd like to challenge you to share what you've learned—or whatever God places on your heart—with others. There are so many people who are hurt, who feel rejected, and just don't see any hope for their future. Let's start taking a stand for Christ! Let's share the *truth* and the unconditional love of Jesus! It's time to stop letting the enemy have his way in our lives.

Rise up and declare, I am a child of the most high God— not because of anything I've done but because of everything He has done! IT IS FINISHED! (**John 19:30**)

I pray that you have enjoyed this *21 Day Freedom Challenge* with God as your tour guide. I encourage you to continue seeking God daily. Allow Him to remind you of this absolute truth—*you are ACCEPTED, CHOSEN, VALUED, AND LOVED by the God who holds the world in the palm of His hand.*

KEY SCRIPTURES
& FREEDOM POINTS

DAY 1: STOLEN IDENTITY—DISCOVERING THE REAL YOU

Key Scriptures:

- *The thief comes only to steal and kill and destroy. I came that they may have life and have it abundantly,* **John 10:10**.
- *For we are God's masterpiece,* **Ephesians 2:10**.
- *I am fearfully and wonderfully made, I know that full well,* **Psalm 139:14**.
- *I am God's child,* **John 1:12**.

Freedom Points:

- You are not defined by your performance, accomplishments, or past mistakes.
- Who you are is not determined by your actions or the opinion of others.
- Who you are is a child of God.
- Your identity in Christ never changes and can never be taken

away from you. Once you're a child of God, you're always a child of God—no matter what!

- We must stop allowing the lies of the enemy to hide the truth of who we are in Christ.

DAY 2: OVERCOMING INSECURITY— IS YOUR HEAD GETTING IN THE WAY OF YOUR HEART?

Key Scriptures:

- *Oh yes, you shaped me first inside, then out; you formed me in my mother's womb. I thank you, High God—you're breathtaking! Body and soul, I am marvelously made!* **Psalm 139:14** (MSG).
- *Before I formed you in the womb I knew you, before you were born I set you apart,* **Jeremiah 1:5.**

Freedom Points:

- Insecurity keeps us from walking in the true identity of who God created us to be.
- When we look to anyone or anything other than God for our acceptance, insecurity rears its head and causes us to go in search of something that will fill the void in our lives and silence the voice that reminds us "we're not enough."
- When we begin to look to God for our acceptance and approval we find that it doesn't require our performance or

perfection, but rather our faith.

- Freedom is found when you step out of the world's definition of beauty and success and step into the transforming power of God's righteousness!

DAY 3: JEALOUSY—IT'S NOT FAIR; I WANTED THAT!

Key Scriptures:

- *You are still worldly. For since there is jealousy and quarreling among you, are you not worldly? Are you not acting like mere humans?* **1 Corinthians 3:3**.
- *For where you have envy and selfish ambition, there you find disorder and every evil practice,* **James 3:16**.

Freedom Points:

- Comparison fuels jealousy and feeds our insecurity.
- Jealousy feeds our insecurity and has a way of forming calluses on our hearts and manipulating our minds.
- Plug into the power source, God's truth. As we begin to allow the truth of God's Word to fill our hearts, the lies of the enemy are exposed.
- Stop comparing ourselves (our appearance or abilities) as well as our circumstantial positions to those around us. God has created us all unique with our own gifts and abilities.

- Develop a grateful heart. A grateful heart has nothing to do with my feelings, but everything to do with God's freedom for my life.

DAY 4: WALLS—TEARING DOWN WALLS FROM YOUR PAST

Key Scriptures:

- *It is for freedom that Christ has set us free. Stand firm, then, and do not let yourself be burdened again by a yoke of slavery,* **Galatians 5:1.**
- *You will know the truth and the truth will set you free,* **John 8:32.**
- *The weapons we fight with are not the weapons of the world. On the contrary, they have divine power to demolish strongholds,* **2 Corinthians 10:4.**

Freedom Points:

- Walls are formed, strongholds are built when we believe and agree with the lies the enemy offers us about our identity, our circumstances, or others in our lives.
- God's Word is the only weapon that will demolish the lies of the enemy and tear down the strongholds in our lives.
- God's truth will transform your thinking in a way that will allow you to begin seeing yourself as God sees you.

- The truth of God's Word has healing power that exposes the lies the enemy wants us to believe and replaces them with a never changing truth that sets us free.
- Your past is never to remind you of your mistakes; it's always to remind you of God's miracles!

DAY 5: DO'S AND DON'TS—I'M SO CONFUSED!

Key Scriptures:

- *Religion that God our Father accepts as pure and faultless is this: to look after orphans and widows in their distress and to keep oneself from being polluted by the world,* **James 1:27.**
- *And I pray that you, being rooted and established in love, may have power, together with all the saints, to grasp how wide and long and high and deep is the love of Christ, and to know this love that surpasses knowledge-that you may be filled to the measure of all the fullness of God,* **Ephesians 3:17-19.**
- *Love the Lord your God with all your heart, and with all your soul and with all your strength and with all your mind; and, Love your neighbor as yourself,* **Luke 10:27.**

Freedom Points:

- How we view God has a direct effect on how we respond to God.
- God's primary desire is to make us like His son and for us to

reflect His character.

- What God wants most from His children is a pure heart, not perfect performance. He wants to be The One you run to for your acceptance and security.
- You don't have to work to earn God's love and approval—it's free of charge! He has an agape love for you and me. It's an unconditional love that never changes.

DAY 6: GOD, IS THAT YOU? PLUGGING INTO THE ULTIMATE POWER SOURCE

Key Scriptures:

- *He who belongs to God, hears what God says,* **John 8:47.**
- *Faith comes by hearing, and hearing by the word of God,*
- **Romans 10:17.**
- *Call to me and I will answer you, and will tell you great and hidden things that you have not known,* **Jeremiah 33:3.**
- *My sheep listen to my voice: I know them, and they follow me,* **John 10:27.**

Freedom Points:

- God still speaks today…through scripture, prayer, dreams, visions, impressions, and words of prophecy.
- It's our awareness of His presence that allows us to hear His

voice. It is by faith that we hear God and it is by faith that we receive the words of God.

- When God speaks, it will always agree with the truth of His Word.
- We can always trust God's Word and His way!

DAY 7: THE FINISH LINE—HOW LONG UNTIL WE'RE THERE?

Key Scriptures:

- *Let your eyes look straight ahead; fix your gaze directly before you,* **Proverbs 4:25.**
- *So we fix our eyes not on what is seen, but on what is unseen. For what is seen is temporary, but what is unseen is eternal,* **2 Corinthians 4:18.**
- *Let us throw off everything that hinders and the sin that so easily entangles. And let us run with perseverance the race marked out for us,* **Hebrews 12:1.**
- *I have told you these things so that in me you may have peace. In this world, you will have trouble. But take heart! I have overcome the world,* **John 16:33.**

Freedom Points:

- Keeping our eyes on where we are going reminds us that where we are isn't our final destination.

- Start running your race with purpose, knowing and believing that God is waiting at the finish line to embrace you with arms wide open.
- It is through our struggles that we encounter God's strength and power to continue the journey. It's in His strength that our greatest victories are won!
- Maintaining our focus on God is the key to walking in victory.

DAY 8: FORGIVENESS—DO I HAVE TO?

Key Scriptures:

- *Be kind hearted to one another, tenderhearted, forgiving one another as God in Christ forgave you,* **Ephesians 4:32**.
- *Bear with each other and forgive one another if any of you has a grievance against someone. Forgive as the Lord forgave you,* **Colossians. 3:13**.

Freedom Points:

- Forgiveness is not forgetting, it is choosing to let go of the offense.
- Forgiveness is not saying that what someone did to you is acceptable. Forgiveness is not giving another permission to mistreat you. Forgiveness isn't getting even with the one that hurt you. Forgiveness is letting God handle the injustice done to you.

- The longer I hold onto an offense, refusing to forgive; the wider the door gets for the enemy.
- Forgiveness releases the person that committed the offense and reboots my heart to a healthy condition.
- Forgiveness starts with a choice and is required of us daily so that we continue walking in the freedom that Christ died to give us.

DAY 9: TAKE IT BACK!

Key Scriptures:

- *Be strong in the Lord and in his mighty power. Put on the full armor of God so that you can take your stand against the devil's schemes,* **Ephesians 6:10-17**.
- *Look, I have given you authority over all the power of the enemy, and you can walk among snakes and scorpions and crush them. Nothing will injure you,* **Luke 10:19**.
- *Be on alert, stand firm in the faith, act like men, be strong,* **1 Corinthians 16:13**.

Freedom Points:

- As believers, the Holy Spirit has equipped you and me to stand against the enemy and his schemes.
- God never intended for us to live a life of defeat. He went to the cross for our freedom. The Bible says that we are more

than conquerors in Christ; we've been given authority in Christ over the power of the enemy, and in Christ, we are children of the Most High God.

- We are in God's army and we must arm ourselves for the battle by putting on the armor of God.
- No longer will we stand back and let Satan have his way in our lives. No more will we allow the enemy to hinder, block or delay the blessings of God.

DAY 10: FEAR—IT'S TIME TO GO!

Key Scriptures:

- *God did not give us a spirit of fear, but one of power, love and a sound mind,* **2 Timothy 1:7**.
- *There is no fear in love. Perfect love casts out (drives out) fear,* **1 John 4:18**.
- *The LORD will keep you from all harm-- he will watch over your life,* **Psalm 121:7**.
- *Greater is He who is in me, than He who is in the world,* **1 John 4:4**.

Freedom Points:

- Fear is one of the greatest tools the devil uses to take our focus off God and brings with it a great deal of uncertainty and doubt about God's character and where God is in our lives.

- When we feel afraid, we can choose to become aware of the fear and ask God where He is and what He wants us to know about the fear OR we can allow the fear to take hold and begin to control our thoughts and emotions.
- The enemy is to be under our feet, not over our circumstances.

DAY 11: SEXUAL PURITY IN A FALLEN WORLD—WHAT'S THE BIG DEAL; EVERYBODY'S DOING IT!

Key Scriptures:

- *Then, after desire has conceived, it gives birth to sin: and sin, when it is full-grown gives birth to death,* **James 1:15.**
- *Do you not know that your bodies are temples of the Holy Spirit, who is in you, whom you have received from God? You are not your own; you were bought with a price. Therefore, honor God with your bodies,* **1 Corinthians 6:19-20.**
- *Flee from sexual immorality. Every other sin a person commits is outside the body, but the sexually immoral person sins against his own body,* **1 Corinthians 6:18.**
- *There is no condemnation for those who are in Christ Jesus,* **Romans 8:1.**

Freedom Points:

- God wants the very best for His children. He has given us things on earth to enjoy, but with those things He has placed certain boundaries around them for our protection.
- If we allow God to direct our steps we will be able to stand our ground against the enemies schemes and glorify God in the process.
- Start today with a decision to honor God with every choice you make.
- When we walk in the truth of God's Word, we no longer feel the need to do things to fit in or to be accepted, because we remember who we are and believe that we already do fit in and are accepted by the only ONE that matters.

DAY 12: ANGER—3, 2, 1 BLAST OFF!

Key Scriptures:

- *In your anger do not sin. Do not let the sun go down while you are still angry, and do not give the devil a foothold,* **Ephesians 4:26-27**
- *Human anger does not produce the righteousness that God desires,* **James 1:20**.
- *Refrain from anger and turn from wrath; do not fret-it only leads to evil,* **Psalm 37:8**.

- *A quick-tempered person does foolish things, and the one who devises evil schemes is hated,* **Proverbs 14:17**.
- *Do not take revenge, my dear friends, but leave room for God's wrath, for it is written: "It is mine to avenge, I will repay," says the Lord,* **Romans 12:19**.

Freedom Points:

- Anger is a God-given emotion; we decide how we will handle this emotion.
- By choosing to hold onto the offense of another, we open the door for the enemy, giving him access to our heart.
- We can either allow anger power over our emotions, which is the same as giving the one who hurt us power, OR we can choose to give the anger to God and ask Him what the truth is about the situation we find ourselves in.
- God will vindicate you. Don't take matters into your own hands—lay all your hurts and anger at the foot of the cross.

DAY 13: GOD'S PERFECT PLAN—SALVATION

Key Scriptures:

- *For God so loved the world, that he gave his one and only son, that whoever believes in him shall not perish but have eternal life,* **John 3:16**.

- *Everyone who calls on the name of the Lord will be saved,* **Romans 10:13**.
- *If you confess with your mouth that Jesus is Lord and believe in your heart that God raised him from the dead, you will be saved,* **Romans 10:9**.
- *Therefore, if anyone is in Christ, the new creation has come: The old has gone, the new is here!* **2 Corinthians 5:17**.
- *For He has clothed me with garments of salvation and arrayed me in a robe of His righteousness,* **Isaiah 61:10**.
- *For it is by grace you have been saved, through faith—and this is not from yourselves, it is the gift of God,* **Ephesians 2:8**.
- *Preach the word; be prepared in season and out of season; correct, rebuke and encourage with great patience and careful instruction,* **2 Timothy 4:2**.

Freedom Points:

- The beauty of salvation is that it doesn't require us to do anything. All that is required is total surrender—exchanging our will for His way.
- Salvation is received, not achieved.
- You have a new identity—you are a new creation in Christ. You are no longer defined by your past, present or future sins.
- Salvation offers us the gift of the Holy Spirit giving us 24-hour access to the God of the universe. There's never a busy signal, you can access the Holy Spirit whenever you call!
- Let what God has done in your life be a reminder of the

power of God. Don't allow the enemy to silence you, stand up and be proud of your heritage, you belong to God!

DAY 14: DEPRESSION, OPPRESSION—WHAT'S THE CONNECTION?

Key Scriptures:

- *The Lord is a stronghold for the oppressed, a stronghold in times of trouble,* **Psalm 9:9.**
- *Why, my soul, are you downcast? Why so disturbed within me? Put your hope in God for I will yet praise him, my Savior and my God,* **Psalm 43:5.**
- *The Lord is a stronghold for the oppressed, a stronghold in times of trouble,* **Psalm 9:9.**

Freedom Points:

- God will reveal to you absolute truth that will expel the darkness in your life.
- When we begin to feel the darkness moving in, we must immediately turn our focus onto the goodness of God and remember that our hope is not in our circumstances. Our hope, is in the Lord and the power of His rising!
- There is no shame in asking for help. Sometimes God heals through doctors and medicine—seek the counsel of the Lord; He will direct your steps.

- Don't allow the enemy permission to steal one more day, take authority over the darkness and bring it into the light—the victory over depression is yours in Christ Jesus!

DAY 15: SECURITY CHECKPOINT—WHAT WILL YOU ALLOW TO COME AND GO?

Key Scriptures:

- *The tongue has the power of life and death, and those who love it will eat its fruit,* **Proverbs 18:21**.
- *A good man brings good things out of the good stored up in his heart, and an evil man brings evil things out of the evil stored up in his heart. For the mouth speaks what the heart is full of,* **Luke 6:45**.
- *Above all else, guard your heart, for everything you do flows from it,* **Proverbs 4:23**.
- *Likewise, the tongue is a small part of the body, but it makes great boasts. Consider what a great forest is set on fire by a small spark,* **James 3:5**.

Freedom Points:

- The words we speak contain power. Our words have the power to build up or tear down.
- What we allow into our heart is reflected in the words we

speak, and directs the path our lives will take.

- Guard your heart and your mind; you are the gatekeeper. Choose your words carefully. When the enemy speaks a lie to you, you counter back with the truth. Confess the truth daily, even if it's completely opposite of the way you feel.

DAY 16: RESTING IN HIM—FREEDOM FROM RELIGION

Key Scriptures:

- *Come to me, all you who are weary and burdened, and I will give you rest,* **Matthew 11:28.**
- *For anyone who enters God's rest also rests from their works, just as God did from His,* **Hebrews 4:10.**
- *Live in Me. Make your home in Me just as I do in you,* **John 15:4** (MSG).

Freedom Points:

- A relationship is built on truth. When we are trusting in God, we can rest knowing that God is at work in our lives, no matter what we see.
- Our relationship with God is not based on us trying harder and doing all the right things...it's about surrender. Exchanging our will for His way.
- God's love is received, not achieved.

DAY 17: FAITH — MY FAITH OR YOURS?

Key Scriptures:

- *Now faith is confidence in what we hope for and assurance about what we do not see,* **Hebrews 11:1.**
- *We will overcome, by the blood of the lamb and the word of OUR testimony,* **Revelation 12:11.**
- *So faith comes from hearing, that is, hearing the Good News about Christ,* **Romans 10:17.**
- *Seek first his kingdom and his righteousness, and all these things will be given to you as well,* **Matthew 6:33.**
- *If you look for me wholeheartedly, you will find me,* **Jeremiah 29:13.**

Freedom Points:

- As believers, we need our own faith—that comes from our own experiences with God—to endure the race that God has set before us.
- If we want to trust what God says is true, we must first know Him.

DAY 18: PRAYER—24 HOURS A DAY, 7 DAYS A WEEK

Key Scriptures:

- *The Lord is near to all who call on Him, to all who call on Him*

in truth, **Psalm 145:18.**
- *Devote yourselves to prayer being watchful and thankful,* **Colossians 4:2.**
- *Pray continually,* **1 Thessalonians 5:17.**
- *Cast your cares on the Lord, for He cares for you,* **1 Peter 5:7.**

Freedom Points:

- Prayer isn't a series of eloquent words, it's an ongoing conversation with the ONE Who knows you best.
- Prayer is spending time with God. There is no right or wrong way to pray. Prayer is opening up your heart, emptying yourself and coming to God in humility.
- Prayer provides the way to transfer the heaviness of our hearts to the faithfulness of God's hands.

DAY 19: THE THREE C'S YOU WILL BE GLAD YOU BROUGHT HOME— CONFIDENT, COURAGEOUS, AND COMMITTED.

Key Scriptures:

- *Am I now trying to win the approval of human beings, or of God? Or am I trying to please people? If I were still trying to please people, I would not be a servant of Christ,* **Galatians 1:10.**
- *Have I not commanded you? Be strong and courageous. Do not be afraid: do not be discouraged, for the Lord your God will be*

with you wherever you go, **Joshua 1:9**.
- *If God be for us, who can be against us?* **Romans 8:31**.

Freedom Points:

- It's time to stand up for what's right, in a world that's gone wrong.
- A godly leader remains Confident, Courageous and Committed by placing their total trust in God.
- Taking a stand for Christ can be spelled **R-I-S-K**. Standing alone can be risky business but when you are standing for Christ you are never standing alone.
- A courageous leader keeps walking even when faced with fear.
- A committed leader doesn't let what he or she sees change what he or she knows to be true about God.

DAY 20: DON'T FORGET WHO YOU ARE

Key Scriptures:

- *Then the Lord reached out His hand and touched my mouth and said to me, "I have put my words in your mouth",* **Jeremiah 1:9**.
- *Every good and perfect gift is from above, coming down from the Father of the heavenly lights, who does not change like shifting shadows,* **James 1:17**.
- *For I am not ashamed of the gospel, because it is the power of God that brings salvation to everyone who believes,* **Romans 1:16**.

Freedom Points:

- My identity is not defined by my mistakes or the opinion of others—my identity is defined by God's truth and He says I matter!
- God is good all the time, even when bad things happen. God's timing is perfect, even when expectations appear unmet.
- I am not EVER to be ashamed or afraid to share the good news of Christ's love—even when faced with opposition!

DAY 21: THE ULTIMATE CHALLENGE!

Key Scriptures:

- *Where the spirit of the Lord is, there is freedom,* **2 Corinthians 3:17**.
- *I know the plans I have for you, plans to prosper you and not to harm you; plans to give you a hope and a future,* **Jeremiah 29:11**.
- *He is the same today, tomorrow and forever,* **Hebrews 13:8**.

Freedom Points:

- Spend time daily allowing God to fill your heart with His truth.
- You are ACCEPTED, CHOSEN, VALUED, AND LOVED by the God Who holds the world in the palm of His hand.

ABOUT THE AUTHOR

Alice Krug has a passion to help parents and teens. This passion is expressed through her ability to encourage others in the knowledge of God's Word. God has placed a mandate on her life to share the freedom of His transforming power—the power to be who God created you to be.

Alice has many years' experience with middle school and high school students as a teacher. Her involvement has gained her first-hand experience and practical knowledge in recognizing and ministering to the needs of parents and teens.

Texas born and raised, Alice has been married for over 20 years to the love of her life, her husband, J.D. They are the proud parents of two amazing, yet completely normal teenagers.

Alice and her family are active members at Gateway Church in Southlake, Texas.

DESTINY WALKING SPEAKING ENGAGEMENT

If you would like to have author and speaker, Alice Krug at your event, you may contact her at *info@DestinyWalking.com*.

Visit Alice's blog at *www.DestinyWalking.com* and her Twitter page *@DestinyWalking*

Other materials by Alice Krug:

* *The 21 Day Freedom Challenge Bible Study For Parents & Teens* (coming soon)